LIMPING BUT BLESSED

Wrestling with God after the Death of a Child

Jason Jones

Fortress Press

Minneapolis

LIMPING BUT BLESSED

Wrestling with God after the Death of a Child

Cover images: Jacob and Jason Jones, © Brea Jones.

Cover design: Brad Norr

Print ISBN: 978-1-5064-0910-8

eBook ISBN: 978-1-5064-0911-5

The paper used in this publication meets the minimum requirements of American National Standard for Information Sciences — Permanence of Paper for Printed Library Materials, ANSI Z329.48-1984.

Manufactured in the U.S.A.

This book was produced using Pressbooks.com, and PDF rendering was done by PrinceXML.

LIMPING BUT BLESSED

CONTENTS

FIRST PERSON FAITH SERIES INTRODUCTION

Theologians often like to claim that *everyone is a theologian*. Still, theology is too often confined to stuffy classrooms and thick books full of footnotes. Meanwhile, everyday people are living their lives, suffering through traumas, celebrating joys, and reflecting on what it all means in relation to God, truth, and belief. In other words, they actually are *doing theology*.

Theology for the People endeavors to make theology relatable and readable, for everyone. And in this, the First Person Faith series, we have sought out authors who have reflected theologically on their lives, even though they are not theologically trained. In church lingo, these are called laypersons. But as you will see, just because they haven't been to seminary doesn't mean they haven't wrestled with meaning at the deepest and most profound levels. They have. And as you read along, we think you will, too.

ACKNOWLEDGMENTS

To the pastors and theologians who have helped me with my questions and doubts over the last few years – thank you for taking the time to provide hope and guidance when I needed it most. Thank you for encouraging, listening, and sitting in our hopelessness with us. You introduced me to a new understanding of God, One who shares in our suffering and One whose love is without conditions.

To Grace Bible Church – You were the first people at our house on the worst day of our lives. I will never forget everything you have done for us. And, I know there are things you did that I don't even know about. Thank you for praying for our family, providing meals, and for showing us grace and love. We are so appreciative to all of you. Know that we love you all deeply.

To our friends – We are so grateful to have had such a supportive network of friends who cared for us and stayed in the trenches with us for so long. I know we were not easy to be around. Thank you for hanging in there. Thank you for crying with us, talking with us, and drinking a lot of wine with us. We know how blessed we are to have you in our lives. We are forever in debt to you.

To Paula Loring – I never thought I would sit in a therapist's office. Ever. You have no idea how grateful I am to have spent three years sitting across from you. The things you taught us will go with us for the rest of our lives. You are a gift from God to all the people you have helped over your career. You walked alongside us, carried our pain and burden with us, and guided us toward hope and healing. I can never thank you enough for what you have done for our family.

To our family – Without you, I'm not sure where we would be today. You kept us alive. Your help and support went above and beyond what anyone would expect a family to do. You literally took control of our lives when we lost all sense of being able to help ourselves. You cared for us. You fed us. You prayed for us. You cried with us. There is no way I could ever say enough about how much it has meant to me and how much it helped us.

I know each of you have grieved Jacob and it has been incredibly painful for all of you. I'm sorry our family has experienced this tragedy. But, I know we will all continue to use that pain and our love for Jacob to do great things. Thank you for always remembering him and keeping him a part of our family.

To Kendall and Kelsey – No father has ever loved his daughters more than I do. You are so strong and beautiful. Your momma and I can't wait to see what huge impact you have in this world. The love and joy you bring me fuels me to be a better man, father, and husband. You are the delights of my life. My girls, thank you for loving me and bringing so much love and laughter in my life. You will always have your daddy's heart.

To Brea – Growing up, I remember wondering what my wife would be like. Never did I imagine marrying the total package. I'm so blessed to have found my soul mate and best friend as a teenager. Our pain and grief over Jacob is not bigger than the love the five of us have for each other. That love will always overcome our circumstances.

You are a warrior for our family. Our family is what it is because of the woman you are. Thank you for fighting so hard for our family. You have prayed harder than anyone that our family would heal and that I would find peace with God again.

The grace with which you walk this path is incredible. I'm eternally grateful for the love, patience, and forgiveness you have extended to me over the years. Only you and I have the same Jacob-sized hole in our hearts. Even though they were steeped in pain, I will forever cherish the sacred moments we have shared the last five years: crying with you in bed, holding you in the kitchen after visiting Jacob's grave, laughing through our tears as we talked about something funny Jacob did, watching the girls play and imagining what Jacob would be doing with them. I'm thankful you have been my suffering partner.

You have always been my light in the darkness. You are the love of my life.

Dedicated to Jacob Thomas Jones – my little man. I am so proud to be your daddy. I've learned to love and laugh harder because of you. Your life has brought so much to this world—more than most men could ever hope for. You will continue to make an impact because of the way you touched our hearts.

I promise to continue to carry your legacy of hope for as long as I live. I'm so grateful to have you as my son and I'm blessed to have spent the time that I did with you. It was too short. However, living a lifetime with a broken heart is worth getting to experience having you as my son for three years.

I miss you so much . . .

INTRODUCTION: JACOB IN THE PRESENT TENSE

My son is dead, but I still think about him in the present tense. When we talk about people who have died we often talk about them in the past tense. I struggle to reconcile this when I talk about Jacob.

It may be semantics, but in my mind Jacob is not gone forever. He is still my son. I didn't *used* to have a son. I have a son. So, when I talk about him, I try to say things like: "He is a sweet fun-loving kid." I know that sounds crazy to other people. Maybe they think that I'm living in denial. But because I believe Jacob continues to be who he is, there is no reason to speak of him using the past tense. I don't want to say Jacob *was* a good boy. I want to say Jacob *is* a good boy. He didn't stop being who he is at the time of the accident.

This is especially true because I believe in a life that comes after this earthly life. And I believe I will be with Jacob again. I don't know or understand what that will look like, but I do have faith that all things will be made new again. For the sake of not confusing you, however, when I talk about Jacob in this book I will use the past-tense verb "was" instead of "is."

This book is about Jacob's life, and his death. It's about what happened on the day of his accident and about what unfolded in the following days, months, and years. And it's about my tenuous, tortured, doubt-filled relationship with God.

You see, God didn't answer my prayers when Jacob died. None of them. They all went unanswered. And to this day, I still experience an overwhelming silence from God.

That doesn't mean I don't believe in God anymore. But I don't believe in him the way I used to.

I don't know if God is.

But I know this: Jacob is.

So maybe God is, too.

MY SUPERHERO

The day we found out we were having a boy, I was full of excitement and joy. I loved playing with dolls and having princess parties with the girls, but I was excited about the new experiences raising a boy would bring—teaching him how to throw a football, fighting with action figures on the living room floor, and watching sports together on Sunday afternoons.

Jacob was delivered via C-section, so when he was born I was only able to get a short glimpse of a fat pasty baby with bright red hair as they rushed him over to a table out of sight. He was a plump little thing with rolls all over and a head full of fine red hair. When he finally blinked his little blue eyes open wide enough, we connected. That was it. This was my son, and I was in love.

Jacob brought a new level of energy to our house. The girls were quiet and well behaved when they played, but Jacob was loud and rambunctious. He was a whirlwind around the house, making noise wherever he went. When he learned how to walk, he stole the girl's high heel dress-up shoes and put them on. From the other side of the house we could hear him, clanking down the hall with those cheap plastic shoes that didn't fit his feet. A typical little brother, he put on their girly costume dress-up clothes and ran through the house laughing because he knew how much it bothered his sisters.

Recently, Brea and I were talking about how much of Jacob's personality had already begun shining through even though he was only three years old. He never reacted to anyone as a stranger and was a happy, contented toddler. He was independent, adventurous, and curious. What stood out to me most was how tenderhearted he was. He loved to cuddle, unlike our daughters, so he got plenty of cuddles from his mommy and daddy. He wasn't shy about giving kisses and big hugs either. He was very affectionate, and everyone that he knew loved that about him.

Jacob was fascinated with superheroes. Every day, he dressed up in a different superhero outfit, or a mix-and-match of a few. Some days he'd wear his cowboy boots, blue jean shorts, and a Batman shirt and mask. When Brea ran errands with him, she often had the protection of Batman or Buzz Lightyear as she walked up and down the grocery store aisle. Brea loves to tell the story of the time when a neighbor's cow got loose and wandered into our front yard. When Brea and Jacob walked outside, the cow started walking toward them, and Jacob put up his arm like Iron Man and started making shooting noises to keep the cow at a safe distance from him and his mother.

Our relationship at first was father and son. But we quickly became playmates, and I often called him my "little buddy." As Jacob got older, building a fort and playing with superhero action figures inside of it was one of our favorite things to do together. He gathered up his action figures and climbed in dressed as a superhero, and we went wherever his toddler imagination would take us.

Our forts were a mess of sheets secured by as many pillows as we could gather and fortified by dining room chairs and the living room couch. I usually played the bad guy and Jacob was the good guy (of course). One of his favorite action figures was Blue Beetle. I'd never heard of him when I was growing up, but he became Jacob's favorite to carry around and play with. Sometimes, out of nowhere, Jacob looked at me and pointed and called me Blue Beetle. Since Blue Beetle was his favorite and he carried him everywhere with him, I took it as a compliment.

I vividly remember a poignant moment with Jacob on one of the many days we spent together in our fort. While we were playing, I asked Jacob if he knew who Jesus was. I don't really know what prompted me to ask my three-year-old this question, but I did. He looked up at me, and he said, "Yes. He's the man at Papa's church." (Papa is the name the grandchildren call my dad.) I put my head down so he couldn't see me laughing at his answer. He was right, though. Jesus was the man at Papa's church. A few weeks earlier, we had gone to an Easter play at my parents' church where we saw a man dressed up like Jesus. We talked a little bit more about the Easter play, and Jacob remembered seeing Jesus go up into the clouds. I'm sure this reminded him of all the superheroes he saw flying around on television. I knew at some point I would revisit who Jesus was, but I wasn't going to confuse him with that explanation at this point. So I moved on.

One of the most special times Jacob and I had together was two weeks before he died. Our family went to a bed-and-breakfast retreat for the weekend with a group of other families. We knew there was a river close by, so we brought fishing poles, including a Spiderman fishing pole for Jacob. He'd never been fishing and was excited to get to use his very own fishing pole, especially one with a superhero on it.

From the time we arrived, he begged me to take him fishing. Honestly, I'm not very interested in fishing, so I kept putting it off. Plus, I didn't expect that we'd catch anything. On our last day, Jacob asked me again about fishing, and I knew I had to take him.

All three of the kids and I walked down to the river and found an open spot in between some trees. We put all of our poles and gear down, I pulled out one of the worms, and I showed them how to put one on a hook. None of them liked that very much and asked me to do it for each of their poles. The kids proceeded to get hooks stuck in trees and broke lines on roots in the water. They didn't know any better and just figured this was part of the deal. After several casts and no bites, Kendall and Kelsey grew tired of it and walked off. I wanted to join them, but Jacob wanted to stay and keep fishing.

While I was baiting a hook on his Spiderman fishing pole he squatted down low to the ground like I did and put his hands on his knees. He patiently watched me put the hook through the worm. He scrunched up his little pudgy nose like he thought it was gross. In the sweetest voice he asked me, "Daddy, are we fishing?" He wanted to make sure we were really accomplishing our goal. I told him, "Yes, Jacob we are fishing."

After casting and casting, to my surprise we actually caught a fish! I was as shocked as Jacob was. "Ha! Jacob, we caught a fish," I told him. I let him reel it in, and he was beaming with excitement. He started laughing at the fish flopping around on the ground.

We both felt pretty proud of ourselves. I can't tell you how glad I am that I took Jacob fishing—it's a memory I will cherish for the rest of my life. It may sound like a very simple story, but it's one of those father-son moments dads dream about. It's even more sacred to me because he died only two weeks later. Thankfully, Brea was able to sneak up behind us that day and take a picture of the two of us to capture the moment. That picture is one of my prized possessions and it's in my office next to me every day.

This book is dedicated to Jacob, my superhero.

1

JUNE 12, 2011

On Sunday, June 12, 2011, after spending a lovely morning on our front porch, our family headed to church. We got the kids dressed, had breakfast, and off we went. Since my wife, Brea, and our girls planned to stay after church to set up for Vacation Bible School, we drove separate vehicles—our son, Jacob, and I would go grab lunch. Then he and I would go home so he could take his afternoon nap.

It was the Sunday that all the kids moved up a class based on their ages. Each Sunday school classroom was named after an animal, and Jacob had been in the Monkey class which consisted of about twenty two three-year-olds. Brea and I sometimes volunteered in there and it was aptly named; with toddlers running around, it was like a zoo. Now Jacob was moving up to the three- and four-year-olds class—the Frog Room.

The change in scenery and new teacher didn't make for smooth drop-off. Jacob started crying and wouldn't stop. I stayed behind and hung out with him until he got comfortable and stopped crying. This was usually a job for Brea, so it was nice to be able to comfort him and sit and play with him until he relaxed. If I'd known what the rest of the day would bring, I would have never left his side.

After church, Jacob and I went to eat at one of our favorite restaurants. It was rare for just the two us to have a meal, so I was happy to get some one-on-one time with him. Jacob had eggs, bacon, and a Sprite; he was excited when I said he could have Sprite with his meal. We talked and laughed all through our meal together.

I was so proud to be his dad. My whole life I had dreamed about having a little boy. I wondered what he would look like. Would he look up to me the way I looked up to my dad? Being a father to a son was something I was especially thankful for. And Jacob was certainly all boy—rowdy, energetic, and adventurous. We often wrestled in the back yard when I got home from work. He'd meet me outside as I drove up the driveway. I could barely get my clothes changed before he made me go outside to play with him. First he wanted me to push him on the swing-set. As I pushed him and he swung back toward me, I tickled his little feet and he'd laugh. He would tell me to stop, but then he'd want me to do it again.

Jacob was a lot like me as a kid—the scrawniest kid in class. When we wrestled, he tried so hard to knock me over. Picking him up and swinging him around took hardly any effort, and we had to be extra careful not to play too rough with him.

It was in these sweet simple moments of playing together that I noticed what a magical bond we had formed as father and son. While I had developed a wonderful relationship with each of my daughters, my relationship with Jacob was different. And as the only two males in the house, we naturally gravitated toward one another.

After leaving the restaurant, I buckled Jacob into his carseat in the back of our SUV and got in behind the wheel. But when I turned the key, the motor didn't turn over. In fact, the ignition made no sound at all. I put my head down in frustration because this had been happening off and on for the last few weeks, and I was afraid the starter had gone kaput. I tried it again; still nothing. Brea was just across the street at the church, so I thought about calling her to come get us. But I waited a few more seconds and then turned the key one more time. This time the engine started right up.

When I look back on moments like this, I think of every little thing that could have gone differently that day. If the SUV hadn't started, for instance, Brea would have given us a ride home. And everything would have turned out differently.

As Jacob and I drove home, he asked me if he could have some M&Ms. I gave him a few but didn't want him to eat the whole bag because he was supposed to take a nap when we got home. Then he started singing along with a song on the radio. "I will follow you." He sang in a sweet quiet voice. "I will follow you." It was the chorus of a song on Christian radio that we'd heard dozens of times.

When we got home, I lay down with Jacob in his bed, and we shared the usual nap routine: lie down with him for a few minutes, rub his back, maybe sing a song or talk a bit, then leave him in his room to rest. When we finished our routine and Jacob was settled, I decided to take a little Sunday-afternoon nap myself.

A couple hours later, I woke up, made some coffee, and flipped on the TV. When Brea and the girls came home, she asked if Jacob was still taking a nap. I said yes. Eventually Brea thought it was getting a bit long for Jacob to be sleeping, so she went to get him up.

This is the moment that my life changed forever.

I heard Brea yelling Jacob's name. I could tell that she was concerned. She came back out and said he wasn't in his room. He didn't answer when she called his name, so the only place we thought he could be was outside. I ran outside and looked in the front yard, and Brea followed. We both yelled his name and looked in all directions around our property. We didn't see him, and he didn't answer us. For some reason, I thought to look inside my SUV—just to rule it out. I ran toward it, with a sinking feeling in my stomach, hoping not to see him.

When I looked in the window, I saw Jacob lying face down in the back of the vehicle, and I instantly felt sick. I tried to open the doors, but they were locked. So I yelled at Brea to get the keys. We finally opened the door, and I pulled Jacob out. His little body was hot, he was limp, and his lips had turned blue.

"GOD, SAVE HIM!"

Brea ran inside to get the phone and called 911. I laid him down in the grass in our front yard and we started doing CPR. I started praying out loud. "God—save him! Please don't let this happen. This isn't happening. Save him. You can save him.

Please!" We had no idea how long he'd been in there, and we still hoped we could revive him. We were not giving up.

The girls ran outside to see us crouched over Jacob doing CPR. In my fear and desire to protect them from what was happening, I yelled at them to go back inside to their room. They turned around and ran back inside, confused and scared. Looking back, I wish I had not yelled at them so loudly. My voice sounded like I was angry, but I wasn't. I was terrified.

While we were doing CPR, I noticed that Jacob's eyes had changed color, from a deep blue to gray. His body didn't feel right either. There was something terribly wrong. His lungs were full of fluid. The sound his chest made when we were doing CPR and the way his eyes looked prompted the worst possibilities to creep into my mind.

Eventually, EMTs showed up and took over the CPR, but I wouldn't leave his side. I held on to Jacob's feet, praying with everything I had inside me. I felt like I was in a nightmare, and I kept thinking, *this can't be real.*

An ambulance pulled up and other EMTs swiftly picked Jacob up and took him inside the ambulance to continue CPR since it was so hot outside. I didn't want to be separated from him, but they wouldn't let me get in the ambulance. It was a moment of staggering helplessness. There wasn't anything I could do for my son. It didn't seem like there was anything I could do to help him but pray. So, that's what I did.

I went to the back of the ambulance, held on to it, and kept praying for a miracle. I distinctly remember saying to God, "This is your chance to do a miracle that everyone will hear about. This is your chance to do something great and everyone will know it's because of you. Please do something, and I will never stop telling everyone what a powerful, good, loving God you are. Please save him now!" Holding on to that ambulance, it felt like everything around me went into slow motion, and I couldn't hear anything around me. I had never prayed so intensely and so desperately. I thought that if God was ever going to answer one of my prayers, this had to be it.

I prayed as hard as a human being could possibly pray.

As time went on, I grew increasingly frustrated because the paramedics wouldn't tell us how Jacob was doing. I wanted to know what was going on, but I couldn't see inside. There was a window on the back, so I climbed up on the bumper to look inside. All I could see were two EMTs sitting beside Jacob, who was covered by a yellow sheet. I lost my mind.

"What are you doing?" I screamed as loud as I could. "What are you doing? Why do you have that over him?" The sheet over his body meant one thing, and I was not ready to accept it. "Don't stop! You hear me! Don't you stop!" I screamed as loud as I could, and I started banging on the back of the ambulance. "Please don't stop. You can't stop! Don't give up on him!"

The sheriff pulled me off the ambulance, and I could tell he was considering restraining me. I stared at him, daring him to try and hold me back.

I thought I was going to vomit. I was confused and dizzy—everything was spinning around me. The sheriff walked over to Brea and me and said that Jacob was gone and that nothing more could be done.

We didn't believe them. How could this be happening to us?

DO NOT TOUCH

Brea and I sat down next to the ambulance in a complete daze, sobbing. This is the moment our hearts broke and our souls were crushed. The dreams we had for our family poured out of our eyes into a puddle on the hot, baked dirt. I felt like someone was pulling my guts out through my mouth.

In that moment, all we wanted was to see our son and to hold him. The sheriff told us we could hold him after the coroner arrived and examined his body, so we would have to wait. He said we could get in the ambulance, but that we could not touch Jacob. We were totally confused and beyond angry. "You mean, we can't even hold our son?" I argued. As any parent can imagine, our only desire was to hold and comfort Jacob. It didn't matter that they told us he wasn't alive. We needed to touch him and hold him. At the very least, though, we needed to see him, so we agreed to not touch him and got into the ambulance.

As we climbed inside, the EMTs and sheriff surrounded us like we were going to steal our son's body. All we could do was look at him. We were in complete shock and stunned by what had happened. The scene was insane and ridiculous. We were sitting inside the ambulance surrounded by a bunch of strangers who forbade us to touch our son—our son who was lifeless right in front of us. I don't know how we kept from grabbing him. I definitely thought about it. Could I fight back all these men long enough for Brea to hold and kiss Jacob one last time? Probably the jail time would have been worth every second. There's a part of me that thinks I owed it to her because I was the one at home with him when this happened. But, then I thought, don't mess this up; all we have to do is wait until the coroner is done and then we can hold him.

I have no idea how long we were in the ambulance. Time stood still and sped by in a blur all at once. Even though each second in there was torture, it wasn't nearly long enough.

The coroner finally arrived. We hoped she would hurry up and do whatever she was going to do so we could see Jacob again and hold him. A friend of ours asked the sherriff if they would please hurry and give us an opportunity to hold Jacob to say goodbye. All they did was tell us we would have to wait. More time passed.

We saw the coroner leave in her vehicle, so we thought, now we can hold Jacob. But the sherriff told us they were taking Jacob away to the coroner's office and that they would have to perform an autopsy. I hadn't even considered this possibility. All I could think about was how they were going to violate his body. His body was precious to me, and I couldn't handle the fact that they were going to hurt him. It was like I was still thinking of Jacob having to *live* through an autopsy. The reality of his death had still not set in.

We had still not been allowed to hold him. After the sherriff told us they were going to take him away, he said, "You won't be allowed to touch him either."

"We won't be able to hold him? What the hell are you talking about? He's my son. Are you serious?" We were devastated and didn't understand. "But, you said we would get to see him and hold him after the coroner looked at him! Why can't we hold him?"

He told us they were opening a full investigation, so no one would be allowed to touch Jacob. For God's sake we needed to tell him goodbye, and I needed to tell him I was sorry. Now I was wishing we had picked him up in the ambulance and disregarded everything they had said to us.

The ambulance drove away with Jacob—carrying his body away down our driveway, the same driveway he and I had driven up only hours before, with him laughing and singing and eating M&Ms. As they took our son away, a tsunami of sadness, grief, and anger enveloped every fiber of my being.

CAN I MAKE IT?

By this point, it had been over an hour since we told the girls to go inside and stay in Kendall's bedroom. A friend had been in the room with them trying to keep them calm. Now, we had to figure out how

11

to tell our seven- and nine-year-old daughters what had happened to their little brother. I have no idea how we got through it.

Brea and I walked into the bedroom and they were both huddled together sitting on the floor. We sat down and told them as best we could what we thought had happened, and that their little brother had died.

Children have a very difficult time comprehending the finality of death. The girls had some emotion, but it was not devastation. Mostly they were in shock and confused. This was their first experience with any family member dying. And for it to be their own brother—it was just too much for their minds to take in. Their little brains went into protection mode. We held them and cried together. We tried our best to keep from completely breaking down in front of them because we didn't want to cause any more harm and trauma than they were already experiencing.

The sheriff asked me to come outside and explain to him the timeline of events that day. I went through what happened, and we went over to the SUV where we'd found Jacob. He asked me how I found Jacob and to recount every detail I could.

I didn't understand why the sheriff couldn't figure out for himself what had happened. This is so simple, I thought. His line of questioning was centered around whether it was possible that I went inside when I got home and forgot Jacob in his carseat. I was so out of my mind that I even started questioning myself. Did I forget him in the car? No. I didn't forget him; I got him out and we went inside together. Jacob's shirt and shoes were in the house where we took them off. Jacob was not in his carseat when I found him, he was lying down in the back. He wouldn't have been able to get out of his carseat because the carseat buckle was too difficult for a three-year-old to unlatch.

But the sheriff kept pushing, probing, and questioning me, and it occurred to me that he didn't believe me. I started getting angry and impatient. Then I told him that I didn't have anything else to say.

Family and friends started arriving, and we met each group on our driveway, holding each other and crying. It was devastating to see the hurt on my parents' faces. They loved Jacob so much. The collective anguish of our family members was terribly painful. This was the moment when my guilt really hit. The sadness and despair I saw in my family members and in Brea triggered the beginning of a hard battle against the accusing voice that tormented me for the next three years. A whisper inside me started blaming myself for the pain and grief everyone was experiencing.

A group of women huddled around Brea and tried to console her as she sat on the couch in our living room. Everyone was crying and no one knew what to say or what to do. I felt panicky, like I was going to crawl out of my skin. For some reason, I felt the urge to pray. So I started praying out loud again. I asked God to give us strength and to heal us. The pain was so great that I just wanted to stop hurting. This was just the beginning, though. I knew we were in for the hardest days of our lives, but I had no idea how hard they would end up being.

I wanted God to take away the pain because I had never felt something so powerful in my life. The depth of the pain terrified me because I wasn't sure I could survive one more minute of it.

As the evening wore on, our heads became more and more fuzzy with grief. Stress hormones coursed through our bodies as our brains tried to protect us from reality.

UNDER INVESTIGATION

Before the sheriff left, he told us a Child Protective Services case worker would be showing up to start their investigation. And that very night we had to talk with another person and go through further questioning. The CPS agent showed up and started asking us questions about what had happened. She asked us about our children and who was going to be staying with us. I was aggravated because she seemed so flippant about the facts and details of the day. She acted like it was a non-event, as if everything was very routine. I wanted to yell at her, "Our child has died! Stop trying to make small talk and get on with whatever you're going to do. And then get the hell out of here!" But all we could do was sit there, numb, and wait for her to get through all of her questions.

At the end of the interview she explained that I couldn't be at home with our daughters by myself until CPS completed their investigation and made a ruling. I was dumbfounded and angry. She asked for names of relatives who could stay with us and be considered guardians.

Talk about kicking you while you're down. Both Brea and I were already reeling with guilt, but now we had a stranger in our home telling us what we could and couldn't do with our own children. It is frightening, when you go through something like this, to find out how much power the authorities have. I'm sure there are plenty of good reasons for Child Protective Services, but our experience with them was terrible and they operated so inefficiently and with no compassion. After an hour of putting us through a grueling interview, the woman left.

By 9:00 p.m. about 20 family members had arrived, and they stayed the night—many of them stayed with us for weeks afterwards. We hadn't eaten anything since lunch, but we couldn't eat. All we did was sit and cry. We cycled from sitting in a numb stupor, filled with shock, to outbursts of uncontrollable crying, to shaking our heads in disbelief.

Physically, I felt nauseous and nervous. My chest was tight—in fact, I had a nagging pain in my chest that didn't go away for months. With deep grief comes a fuzzy mind and inability to focus. We were still denying this had happened to us.

For the first time in my life, I wanted to die. It felt like it would be impossible to live without my son. I had never questioned whether I could make it through something in my life, until now. The pain seemed like it was too much to bear. And the physical symptoms of grief made it nearly impossible to function. I asked my brother and sister multiple times, "How am I going to make it? Do you think I can do this? I don't think I can." I trusted them to be honest with me when I couldn't trust my own feelings. They told me I could make it, but also they told me I didn't have a choice: "You have to make it," they said. "The girls need you, and Brea needs you."

Honestly, in that moment, I didn't think the rest of my family needed me. The pain warped any good sense I had. I was living in a cloud of despair that left me barely able to breathe. "Hadn't I caused all this pain in the first place?" I thought. "They would be better off without me anyway." Not living anymore was a way out of this pain. All I wanted in the moment was to be with Jacob and not to feel this heartbreak. Dying seemed like a good alternative to living with my guilt and grief.

Getting into bed that night seemed unnatural and wrong. "What am I doing? Going to sleep? I can't sleep." I closed my eyes and thought that maybe there was a chance that this was all a dream. So I lay there somewhere in between reality and a nightmare, not knowing which side I would wake up on. "Please God, by some miracle fix this, and let it not be true when I wake up."

We were exhausted, but so much adrenaline was pumping through us that it was impossible to sleep. It felt wrong even to try to sleep, like I didn't deserve any rest. There's no way I was going to let myself get any relief from what was happening to me. I felt like I deserved whatever pain I was feeling. The least I could do is feel and hold this pain as the beginning of my penance.

As Brea got into bed, we didn't say anything to each other. Our faces must have aged ten years in just a few hours. Our eyes were bloodshot and our brows furrowed, wincing at the looping question in both our minds: Is this really happening? We both cried off and on all night. My sadness turned into a violent flailing, sometimes to the point where I couldn't catch my breath. At times it felt like I was about to pass out from crying so hard. In these early days of grieving, I thought that the fits of crying would never end.

Brea and I cried next to each other but couldn't comfort one another like before. We were used to holding each other and helping each other when we were sad. This was different. We were both so destroyed inside that we had nothing left for each other. With each breath I struggled to keep the last thread of sanity inside me from snapping. It felt that any moment I could lose myself. So we lay there helpless and hopeless, together in the same room but totally alone inside ourselves.

I don't know if I ever fell asleep or not. When morning came, I got up and went into the kitchen hoping to find an empty house and hoping it had all been a bad dream. As I turned the corner, I saw all of my family. The nightmare was real and I had no idea how I was going to make it.

2

STILL WAKING UP

We've all heard the heartbreaking stories of children being accidentally left in carseats by distracted parents, and of those children dying from heat stroke. From the moment the authorities showed up at our house on June 12, they treated me like I had left Jacob in the car. The investigation was yet another level of stress taking place while we tried to figure out how to live with our grief. It was a nightmare within a nightmare.

Over the first several months, we simply tried to survive our grief and to endure the unexpected fight we found ourselves in—a fight for our rights as parents and a fight to prove my innocence.

The day after the accident, our house was full of people. Someone said there were television vans driving back and forth past our house and up and down our road; one stopped in front of the house. I felt disgusted; I felt like our family was being exploited. I was furious to think about a stranger talking about Jacob's death, or talking about him at all. His life is sacred, and I wanted to preserve that.

Stories of families experiencing intense loss are on the news every day. But, until it happened to our family, I had never considered the total violation of privacy and dignity in these sorts of stories. Why are we so interested in the death of people? Why do we think we need to know how someone died? The fact that we pay so much attention to the bad that happens to others is a sad reality in our culture, but I don't understand how the media doesn't have more compassion for people in times of tragedy and trauma. We felt helpless as the story gained media attention and we lost control over our privacy.

The morning of June 13, the lead investigator called my cell phone and asked to come back by the house to finalize his interview with me. He was cordial and said they only needed to wrap up some loose ends. It sounded like it was a harmless non-confrontational meeting, and it was my under-standing that I wouldn't have to talk with them any further. I agreed to meet with him that afternoon.

I didn't know at the time, but my family had

spoken to an attorney. Right before the scheduled time the investigators were to arrive, my brother and brother-in-law told me that an attorney had advised us not to meet with anyone else without an attorney present. The attorney said that we lived in a very aggressive county and he was afraid they would try to prosecute me for child negligence. We needed to hire a defense attorney before we talked with authorities again. It hadn't even occurred to me that I'd been criminally negligent.

My brother and brother-in-law walked down our driveway to meet the investigators when they arrived. They spoke for several minutes, and then the investigators drove off. When they got back up to the house, I could tell that something was wrong. With the rest of my family gathered around, my brother said that one of the investigators wasn't sure I was telling the truth. He told them they wanted to meet with me again to give me the opportunity to tell the truth. In short, they thought I was lying.

Fear and anxiety set in when we started thinking about the possibility of having to fight this legally. I couldn't fathom why the legal system would pursue parents after an accidental death of a child. Don't they realize there is no guilt or punishment they could heap on us that we weren't already doing to ourselves? Suddenly, on top of my grief, I was worried about going to jail.

A Mountain of Guilt and a Lie Detector Test

The accusations deeply affected Brea as well, and I was concerned for her mental health. Not only was she having to think about Jacob, but she was having to question whether her husband was going to be prosecuted. And her anxiety added to the mountain of guilt I was already carrying. I wanted her to be able to grieve fully for Jacob and not to worry about what was going to happen to me.

A week after Jacob's accident, I was in an attorney's office going through the events of that day again. My family had hired a criminal defense attorney. I'd never been arrested in my life, and now I was sitting in a law office talking about defending myself from being prosecuted for criminal child negligence. I felt sick to my stomach. To the lawyer, it was just another case. He was rather matter-of-fact about the law surrounding the events of that day and whether anyone could prove I was negligent.

Thankfully, my dad, brother-in-law, and father-in-law went to the meeting with me to support me and to help me through it. I recounted every detail

I could remember about that day and the timeline of events. Once he finished interviewing me, the lawyer said he was going to talk with the sheriff's investigators to see what direction the investigation was going.

A few days later he called. He said that he had talked with the sheriff's office, and the lead investigator didn't think I was telling the truth. So the attorney thought I should take a polygraph test. He said it would go a long way in proving that I was telling the truth—it would be proactive, and it would push things in the right direction. After talking it through with my family, I agreed. Three days later, my dad and sister drove me to take the test.

I was incredibly nervous and my stomach was in knots. I wasn't afraid of failing the test. I was afraid of having to recount the details once again, to relive each painful moment. I was angry that I even had to take the test in the first place. The shock to my body and mind caused by grief affected me so much physically and emotionally, I could barely do more than walk and sit. My mind was in a deep fog and even talking was totally exhausting.

The attorney met us at the office where I was to take the test. When we walked inside, he went straight into a private meeting with the person who was going to administer the polygraph. They were in there for about half an hour. It seemed like an eternity. With every passing second my anxiety and stress level went up. "How long is this going to take? I just want to get this over with," I thought. My sister did her best to calm me. God bless her and my dad for being there. I don't know how I would have gotten through that day without them.

Finally, my attorney came out and brought us into the room where they were meeting. The administrator said he was sorry I was there and he was sorry for what happened to Jacob. Then he said, "There's no way I'm giving you this polygraph test. Your son passed away just a week ago, and your body is not going to give an accurate reading. So, I'm not doing it."

I was relieved to not have to take the test, but I was also furious with my attorney. We were paying this guy a small fortune, and he should have had enough experience to know the test wasn't going to work under these circumstances. It created an enormous amount of stress for me and my family and had been a complete waste of time. We left knowing we were back in the waiting game with the investigator and hoping something would convince him I was telling the truth and close the case.

MORE QUESTIONS, FOR ME AND FOR GOD

A week or so later, I got a call from the investigator. He told me the coroner had provided her results and that my timeline didn't match up with her report. He said that based on the food digestion of Jacob's breakfast, Jacob had eaten earlier than I had indicated in my statement. I was dumbfounded. Jacob and I went to eat after church around 10:30 a.m. The coroner stated that it was closer to 8:00 a.m. I told him that their report was wrong and somehow her findings were incorrect. I told him I wasn't lying and suggested he interview the people at the restaurant and the waitress who knew us and could confirm when we ate.

Just as the investigators were questioning me, I was questioning God. God knew I hadn't done anything wrong. He knew that I was telling the truth. I didn't understand why God wouldn't make the legal troubles go away. Brea and I prayed about it every day, and every day it only got worse.

I began to get really confused with God. It felt like God was letting us down by not "fixing" our situation. We were in so much pain, and it seemed like this was one of those times that God could give us some relief, knowing we were at the end of our rope. As days passed, God's silence became the bricks that started building the wall between me and faith. I felt like we deserved more concrete signs or answers, or something—anything!—to know that God was present in all of this mess. I was really trying to reach out and find comfort from God, like I was taught my whole life and had read in the Bible. Instead, I was overwhelmingly lonely and empty.

Weeks went by with questions back and forth from the attorney to the sheriff's investigators. Eventually, I got a call from the attorney saying the investigators wanted to come by the house for a face-to-face interview. He said they wanted to do one final interview before they made their recommendation to the district attorney on whether to prosecute me or not. We were ready to do whatever it took to put this behind us, so we told the attorney to set it up as soon as possible.

One evening two deputies, my attorney, my sister, Brea, and I sat around a table in our living room. Once again, I was full of nerves, scared of the unknown, and just under the surface I was seething with anger at these investigators who kept dragging us through hell. My heart was broken and I was missing Jacob, but I still had to put my grief on hold so I could get through this investigation.

The lead investigator started the meeting: "I

know you gave a statement on the day of the accident, but I think it's time you tell us all what really happened that day. I'm not sure that we're getting the truth."

Those words pierced right through whatever thin sheet of composure I had. I envisioned jumping across the table and grabbing him by the throat and beating the crap out of him. All of the rage I had toward this investigator boiled right up to the surface in that moment.

"I have told you the truth from the very beginning and I don't know what else to do," I told him, my voice getting louder with each word and trembling with emotion. I started crying tears of anger, and I slowly started standing up out of my chair leaning slightly toward him. Brea put her hand on my leg, pushing me back down into my chair. She didn't say anything, but I got the message. I knew I was losing control—but I was done. I'd had enough. I don't know what else I said, but I sat all the way back in my chair and looked at both the investigators, intentionally not breaking my stare.

After a few silent moments the lead investigator said, "Okay, that's all I needed. I believe you." I was shocked. The message was pretty clear: they were there to push my buttons and to see what came out. The lead investigator told me he would recommend that they drop the case. Before my attorney left that evening, he said he felt good about the direction the case would take and that it should be over soon. I was finally relieved. I could get on with grieving.

Unfortunately that wasn't case. A week or two later, I got a call from my attorney saying that the district attorney was taking my case before the grand jury. I couldn't believe it. When I heard those words, I feared the worst. But our attorney explained that it was the only way the case could ever be completely closed. If the DA didn't let it go to the grand jury, then it could be opened up years later for any reason. I didn't like it, but there wasn't anything we could do about it. It was going to be a couple more months of waiting with this hanging over our head.

Meanwhile, there was a separate investigation underway from Child Protective Services. They dragged their feet on their investigation and they rarely communicated with us. Dealing with CPS was one of the most stressful and infuriating things we had to go through. We knew how we raised our children and that we were good parents. We just wanted to get on with our lives, but they wouldn't meet with us or release us from the investigation. Months had gone by and I was still restricted from being alone with the girls. Finally, CPS said they wanted to interview the girls before they would close the investigation and make a determination. The interview had to be with the girls, in private. We were not allowed to be in the room. We weren't happy about this, but after reviewing the questions, we approved them and set up the meeting. Our goal was just to get this behind us.

At the CPS office, they took the girls back to be interviewed with an attorney present. They interviewed them together and then separately. When they came out, the girls seemed fine and unaffected by the experience. The attorney said they did great and the interview went well, even though they asked the girls questions about physical abuse, which we had not approved. Finally, the CPS investigation was closed, but we were still waiting on the grand jury trial.

After several months, the case with the county finally went to a grand jury. The grand jury returned the decision and "no-billed" the case. Essentially, that meant the case was not going forward with prosecution. It was a huge weight lifted off all of our shoulders.

No God, No Peace;
~~Know God, Know Peace~~

After months of cops and CPS workers and district attorneys questioning my character and my actions, reading stories about our case in the paper and watching TV news vans passing our house, I had internalized a massive amount of guilt. My actions and decisions on June 12, 2011 affected all the people I loved and cared about the most. I started to believe that I was not worthy of being a husband and father.

I became so depressed that I wanted to die. Even though I had people around me telling me it wasn't true, I wondered if Brea and the girls would be better off without me. I felt that I was to blame for the pain and sadness they were experiencing. Day after day, I woke up feeling like there was no hope, and I couldn't imagine ever finding joy again.

I filled my journal with prayers during this time asking for God to give me some peace. For months, I tried to do what I had in the past to help me get through my hardest times, but this was so different and so much worse than anything I had ever been through. I asked God for peace and to help me understand why this had happened, but the pain never subsided and the guilt only got worse. As more time went by, I got angry at the lack of answers, the lack of comfort. I had questions *for* God, and increasingly I had questions *about* God.

For the first six months after the accident, I was using the faith toolkit that I had assembled over my life. I used every tool I could come up with—scripture, prayer, belief—to ease my pain and to answer questions. But one day, I simply ran out of tools. My faith started crumbling as bitterness and doubts mounted against the God I thought I knew.

"God, why did you let this happen? How could a God who is in control let my son die alone in a hot car? How can I ever trust a God like this again?" I asked God to help me with these questions, and I prayed to get answers more times than I can count. Eventually, with no answers, I became angry and bitter.

If one of my children had been crying out for me to help them, I would run to them. I wouldn't ignore them. I would pick them up and hold them. My prayer was that God would do that for me. But instead I felt alone, and I didn't find the God I prayed for. Or God didn't find me. I don't know which. It forced me to question whether God is real at all. And it forced me to question the spirituality and faith I had practiced my entire life.

Everything around me had fallen apart. My son

was gone and I felt like I had let him down when he needed me most. My daughters were in pain and confused by the death of their little brother. My wife was devastated, and I couldn't fix her pain. I hated myself and didn't want to live. And, the God I had hoped in was not helping me find peace when I needed it most.

I had no idea how I was going to survive this, much less put the pieces of my life back together. So, I had a choice to make: keep going or give up. Somehow, each morning I found a reason to keep going rather than give up. There was no magic moment or an epiphany that made everything better. I was living one hard minute at a time.

I heard a story about another grieving parent who was asked how they got through the death of their child. She said, "I didn't. I simply kept waking up."

3

THE GUILT

I cannot describe the guilt and despair of feeling that my actions had caused the death of my child. It overwhelmed and suffocated me for years. Even though part of me held on to the guilt to pay a kind of penance for my actions, at the same time I wanted to break free from what felt like an insurmountable and lifelong burden.

You know that dream we've all had of being chased by a monster or a bad person, running as fast as possible, but not moving at all? That's what it felt like. I was trying with everything inside me to get away from this feeling, but I wasn't able to get anywhere. It left me feeling hopeless and exhausted.

The physical separation from Jacob was deeply painful in and of itself. Unfortunately, my guilt also made me feel like I had lost an emotional connection with my son. It felt like we were separated not only physically but also relationally. When I wanted to think about and remember him, the guilt hijacked the moment and forced me into a tailspin of self-hate. I wanted so badly to hold Jacob peacefully in my mind and heart without having these feelings, but I couldn't.

Reading back through my journal, in nearly every daily entry I apologized to Jacob. Here's an excerpt from October 24, 2011:

> *Jacob, Daddy misses you so much. I've been thinking about you all morning. I wish I could have been holding you to comfort you when you needed me. I'm so sorry I wasn't there to protect and comfort you. I wish there was something I could do to change all of this. Please forgive me.*

I desperately wanted to think of Jacob and to remember what it was like to hold him and talk to him. I wanted to grieve him and just be sad. But as soon as I would think of him or look at a photo of him, I started sinking in quicksand, full of despair and grasping for forgiveness that I couldn't seem to find.

My reactions to the heaviness of the guilt manifested in some strange ways. One of my friends noticed that I didn't say Jacob's name for almost two weeks after the accident. When talking about Jacob, I referred to him as "him" or "he" but I wouldn't say his name. I wasn't doing it consciously, but looking back, I think I refused to say his name as a way of protecting myself from falling apart in conversation. I couldn't bear to say his name because the guilt sent me into such a downward spiral.

For nearly three years, I also had the hardest time looking at pictures of Jacob. I couldn't look at a picture of him without it taking my breath away. Catching a glimpse of him for more than a couple seconds sent me into an episode of uncontrollable crying. When I looked at his sweet little face and tiny body, I told him how sorry I was and that I should have been there to help him. The pictures caught me when I least expected it and sent me into a crumbling mess at home, in his room, in my car, in my office at work, and at the cemetery. It was so bad that we had to strategically place pictures in the house so I was able to avoid them. We even had to ask my parents to take down pictures of Jacob in their house when we visited because it was so painful to see them.

My heart sank the night I went to a group for bereaved parents and they asked me to bring pictures of Jacob to share with everyone. To most parents, it was a special time of sharing about their kids, and you could see the pride in their faces as they looked at pictures and recounted memories. When they asked me to do it, I refused. It wasn't because I didn't want to talk about Jacob but because I didn't want to carry pictures of him, get them out of an envelope, and accidentally see his beautiful smile. The guilt really had incredible power over me, and I didn't know how I was going to get it under control.

I felt like a disappointment as a father and husband. Of all the things to be doing when one of my children needed me, I was sleeping. I was supposed to be there, to help him, to protect him. Instead I took a nap! I felt like I let Jacob and the rest of my family down. I questioned whether I was worthy of being Brea's husband and Kendall and Kelsey's father, though none of them ever made me feel like they held me responsible for Jacob's death.

Everyone around me had forgiven me or didn't place any blame on me for Jacob's accident, except for one person: me. I blamed God for allowing this to happen, and I blamed myself for having fallen asleep and not locking the doors to the SUV. I had no idea how I would ever find any peace. Thankfully, a random referral to a grief counselor turned out to be one of the most important steps in finding a way forward.

JUST KEEP BREATHING

Almost immediately we had people telling us how important it would be for all of us—the girls included—to get into some form of counseling to help us get through our grief. We had no idea how important it would end up being to our survival, and ultimately, our entire family's ability to find a new normal.

One of the pastors at our church told us of a grief therapist he had worked with in hospice care. He asked if he could give her our phone number, and we didn't hesitate in saying yes. Within a few days after the accident, I received a voicemail from a woman who said "Hi, Jason. My name is Paula Loring. First, I want to say how sorry I am and that you all are in my thoughts and prayers. When you're ready, you can give me a call and set up a time to come in. Until then you need to make sure that you are drinking as much water as you can. And, make sure you eat a little bit every day. Other than that, just keep breathing and give me a call if you need anything. Take good care of yourself. Bye."

This call was a breath of fresh air and gave me a sliver of hope when it felt like I was drowning in hopelessness. Knowing there was someone out there who might be able to help us find ourselves again gave us some faith that this wouldn't destroy us.

What seemed like such quick simple advice from Paula over the phone turned out to be incredibly helpful in getting us stable enough to function at a basic level. Under duress, the body releases cortisol and adrenaline, the primary stress hormones, through our bodies, which can lead to dehydration. Drinking a lot of water can help rid the body of the toxins our grieving bodies were creating. Brea and I didn't feel like eating most of the time because our nerves made us so nauseous. We had to make a conscious effort to force some food into our mouths at various points in the day.

Additionally, neither one of us could sleep. Thankfully, a doctor who went to our church was able to get us in to see him very quickly. He gave both of us some sleep aids and anxiety medication. I didn't care what I had to take as long as it gave some relief.

About three weeks after Jacob's death, we walked into Paula's office for the first time. It was surreal. Paula turned out to be an absolute godsend. She was empathetic and let us spill our guts about how we were feeling. We didn't have to hide how hopeless we felt, and we could tell her anything without any judgment from her. Sitting with one person after another in their most painful moments certainly takes a special person, and Paula was a vital part of my healing personally, our healing as a married couple, and our parenting of two girls who were also grieving.

For several months Brea and I went to therapy together, and we talked with Paula about our feelings and what we were dealing with in the moment. Couples therapy was especially helpful because we could hear what each other was feeling and have Paula talk us through our personal issues while the other was sitting there listening. It took the burden off the other spouse in a time when neither of us had much to give the other. It also gave us space to freely talk about what may have been bothering us about one another.

Every person deals with grief differently. One of the initial and most helpful pieces of advice Paula gave us was to let the other person grieve however they wanted to, as long as they weren't hurting themselves or another person. If we needed to go a little crazy, then we were allowed to do it without judgment. Throw something, break something, scream at the top of your lungs, whatever you needed to do that you thought would help you grieve; it was all fair game.

Many marriages break up after the death of a

child. One of the biggest causes of arguments and disagreements stems from judgment of how the other spouse is handling their grief. One person will want to talk about how they feel, while the other one doesn't want to talk about it all. One person wants to cry, while the other doesn't want to show any emotion at all. Eventually, an argument ensues, and it can get messy very quickly.

After a few weeks, I started going to see Paula on my own. She could tell that I was harboring a lot of guilt and recommended that I come see her individually to work through it. I had no idea how long I would end up needing to go to therapy. I imagined it would be a few weeks or at most a few months. But, as time went on, I benefited so much from it that I wondered if I would ever stop going.

I went to therapy nearly every week for the first year after Jacob's death. Thankfully, my colleagues at work told me to take whatever time I needed off from work to get better. When Paula and I met, the issue I had looking at Jacob's pictures kept coming up. After discussing how it was affecting me, she asked me if I wanted to be able to look at his pictures without falling apart. "Of course," I said. I wanted to be able to look at my son's pictures and to find joy in seeing him, like any other parent.

BUZZING MY GUILT

Paula suggested a type of therapy known as Eye Movement Desensitization and Reprocessing Therapy (EMDR). In a typical EMDR session, Paula asked me about a negative belief I was having about myself. For example, a common negative belief I had was that I was a bad father and that I had let Jacob down.

Then Paula would ask me what positive belief I wanted to have about myself regarding that issue. Sometimes the positive belief came easily; other times it was hard to discern. I generally don't have great self-esteem, so I often struggled to come up with something positive about myself. When I eventually did, she had me concentrate on those for a moment.

Paula also asked me how I was feeling physically. At times, I was nervous and had butterflies in my stomach. But, most of the time in these sessions I had a tightness and tension in my chest. It almost felt like someone was sitting on my chest.

While Paula and I discussed how I was feeling in my body and about the beliefs I was having about myself she asked me to grab two small hand-held vibrating devices which buzzed back and forth in my hands. I concentrated on the negative belief and I had different experiences every time. Sometimes

I envisioned myself back in a childhood scene, or a horrific moment the day of Jacob's accident; sometimes I saw words flashing up in front of me.

The guilt was smothering me and controlling my thoughts. Paula quickly connected the dots from my feelings about myself to my inability to look at Jacob's pictures. Looking at his pictures brought all the guilt I was carrying to the surface, causing me to ask him for forgiveness. Many times I lay in his bed holding his picture and sobbing, begging for his forgiveness.

On a number of occasions during my EMDR sessions, Jacob "showed up"—I imagined him in a scene or he came into my imagination, and we interacted in some way.

Once, Paula had me focus on one of my biggest fears. I was so scared and horrified at the amount of pain and fear Jacob must have experienced. All I could think about was how I was lying down in my bedroom probably twenty feet away from him while he was dying in an SUV. I was so close to him, but I didn't know he needed me. Paula asked me to pick up the vibrating devices and start thinking about that scene. I closed my eyes and I could vividly see Jacob in our white Ford Expedition, panicking when he realized he couldn't find a way out. My heart started pounding as I thought of him yelling,

"Daddy! Help me!" I thought about how scared he must have been when he didn't see me coming outside to help him. I saw him put his hands on the window, yelling and crying and needing me to come help him. But I couldn't hear him.

Next I imagined going outside and finding Jacob. But when I pulled him out, he was alive. He was sleeping peacefully. All I wanted to do is hold him, which is what I had longed to do for months. I cradled his head in my arm and leaned his face against my shoulder. I put my face down into his hair and took a deep breath. Then I walked down our gravel driveway with Jacob. I held his sweet little hand.

Getting to walk down the driveway with Jacob like we had done so many times before was a dream that I didn't want to end. We were together again and it felt like the right time to tell him how sorry I was that this had happened him.

In my imagination, I picked him up and looked him in the face and told him I was so sorry and I loved him. I told him that I would have done everything I could to help him if I had only known what was happening to him. I told him I missed him so much and how proud I was to be his daddy. We looked at each other for a few seconds and he smiled and said, "Okay Daddy, can we go play now?" I was surprised at that response. I didn't say anything and I just set him down. He turned around and ran off into the field in front of the house.

This was one of the most profound EMDR sessions I had. I was spilling my guts out to Jacob, asking him to forgive me; he responded by asking to go play. He let me apologize, and then he was ready to move on to other things, just like a three-year-old would.

I don't know how to explain the science of what happened within my brain during that therapy session, but it helped to replace a deeply disturbing and traumatic experience in my mind with a more healing experience, which I now think about as though it really happened. These sessions were some of the most spiritual experiences I've ever had. I can't help but believe that Jacob was with me in some way through that session. It felt like I was truly feeling him and that I was having an encounter with him.

After that session, Paula and I laughed at the way Jacob responded. I know it was my brain working to heal that memory. But in my heart, I believe there was more going on—especially given the amount of healing it eventually led to.

My guilt didn't instantly go away after this one session. It took dozens of EMDR sessions before the negative feelings started to subside. But that day was a big step forward in my healing.

HOT YOGA? WHY NOT?

For over a year I took various medications to help me sleep and deal with anxiety and depression. Once I decided to try to stop taking them, I began to have very uncomfortable withdrawal symptoms. They were so intense, I wanted to crawl out of my skin. I didn't know what to do with myself. I would fidget and wished I could take off sprinting because my body felt like it was going to explode from the inside.

Because the symptoms were primarily physical, I figured that movement or exercise would help reduce the feelings I was having.

On a whim, I thought about trying out hot yoga. I was desperate to try and get rid of these physical symptoms, so I was willing to try anything and everything.

When I walked into the room for class, I could feel the heat, but it wasn't too bad. The room was packed and everyone was lying on their backs.

As we began class, I saw the instructor walk over to the thermostat and turn it up. Then the heater kicked on and hot air began to pump into a room full of people already sweating.

It started getting a little more uncomfortable and I realized I had too much clothing on. A few minutes later, I was in a full-out sweat and breathing hard and we hadn't even gotten up off the floor yet.

About two-thirds of the way through class, I was almost out of water, dizzy from the heat, and I didn't think I could make it. No one else had gotten up to leave, and I didn't want to be the only one who couldn't take the heat.

I had to lie down, though. I concentrated with everything inside myself to keep from throwing up. I hadn't been praying much, but I prayed to keep from passing out in that room.

The hot yoga turned out to be much more of a workout than I imagined. It was like nothing else I had ever tried, yet it did get me to a point of total exhaustion and took my mind off the weird feelings I was having from the withdrawals.

I decided to try it again the next week and see if it was something I could keep doing and continue to benefit from.

During my second class, sweating, feeling uncomfortable and a little woozy, I flashed to thinking about Jacob in the SUV. My mind was still in a pretty vulnerable state during this time, and it wasn't easy for me to control my thoughts or feelings. At the drop of a hat, I could break down.

I started thinking about how Jacob must have felt in the car, compared to my own physical discomfort at this moment. At least I knew I was able to get up and walk out if I needed to. But he was stuck, and it must have been a horrific experience for him.

I wonder if I put myself through this in order to feel some of the same effects Jacob felt in the car. Something inside wanted to put myself through the pain he went through. It may have been me feeling like I needed to pay a penance. I needed to suffer and feel pain like he did in order to understand what he went through and also to suffer with him. But my discomfort was nothing compared to his because I was able to end mine when it became too much, and I didn't experience the fear he did.

All I could do in the moment was try to stop thinking about it and try to concentrate on something else. For a few moments, I thought I was going to have to get up and leave because it just seemed too much.

If I hadn't been in therapy and able to talk through this with Paula, I'm sure it would have been a trigger and I wouldn't have been able to go back. Having the time to talk through and to face the fear head-on instead of running away from it, helped me to keep from focusing on it and making it an issue.

Being routinely active got me out of my head and

into movement, which is tremendously beneficial for anyone struggling with depression. Even if I felt like everything else in my life was out of control, for thirty minutes to an hour, I could get my body moving and I didn't have to think. It was the one time every day that I had control over my body.

LOSING JACOB, LOSING GOD

Even after five years, it's still very hard to imagine that I won't see Jacob again in this life. Thinking about living without Jacob for another forty years wrecks me, so I don't focus on the time that I won't have with him—it's just too painful. While I sometimes want to crawl into a hole and feel sorry for myself and our family, instead I choose every day to focus on what Jacob's love and life will continue to do even though he isn't here. I choose to remember the moments that I did have with him. Those times were precious, and I force myself to focus on the hope of us being together again.

Eventually, I was able to start looking at Jacob's pictures without falling apart. It took around three years to get to that point, and it's still not an easy thing to do. Now when I look at his pictures I might cry, but it's not related to my guilt. My tears are tears of sadness because I miss my boy. There are times when I simply enjoy how beautiful he is, and I remember where we were in the moments we captured on camera.

I still feel like I let Jacob down, but I'm able to bear the guilt and carry it with me instead of it having so much power over me. At some point, I realized that I had to stop fighting the blame I was putting on myself and to accept the fact that I had some responsibility in what happened to Jacob. Of course I didn't cause it or mean for it to happen. It was an accident, and accidents happen to everyone. Unfortunately, this accident caused Jacob's death. There is nothing I can do about it now except to do the best I can with each day, grieve my son, and love and take care of my family.

Therapy helped me break down the wall of guilt between Jacob and me. The connection between the two of us was no longer being smothered by my negative beliefs and feelings about myself. Now, when I think of Jacob or see a picture of him, I am able to hold his memory in peace and full of love.

As my guilt has subsided, it's made room for the other stages of grief. And when I think about not seeing him for so long, I look with hope and faith to life after death. I have no idea what that will look like, but I live with hope for the day Jacob and I will be together again. When I started doubting the existence of God because of the accident, I contemplated what it would be like not to see Jacob again, and that thought terrified me. So I prayed for God to give me a sign and to let me know that Jacob was okay and that we would be together again. But I didn't get the sense of peace or understanding I was looking for. I was desperate for some reassurance, and it seemed like God was out to lunch. God's silence didn't make any sense to me.

Along with Brea, I had been caring for and parenting Jacob day and night for three years, and now our son was gone. I wanted definitive proof that Jacob was okay. It was incredibly frustrating not to feel like God was giving me the assurance I wanted or felt I deserved. The least God could do for us was give us confirmation that there was some purpose or reason for this happening to Jacob.

Imagine if your child was in the front yard playing and you were inside and you heard them screaming your name and wanting you to help them. What would you do? Any good loving parent would run to them, pick them up, and give them the comfort they are seeking. I thought God's reaction was like a parent who just stands at the door watching their child scream at them, doing nothing. That wouldn't be an example of a loving or responsible parent. In fact, it's the opposite—it's cruel, and it's abusive.

I had cried out to God with a broken heart, wanting to know that I would see Jacob again and to get some comfort surrounding our circumstance. Days and months passed and my doubts and questions only grew. Was I asking too much of God? I certainly didn't think so.

Even though I had been given some relief with the guilt I was feeling through therapy, I still wanted to know that I would see Jacob again. This hope was waning with each day as God felt more distant and I understood less about how an all-loving, all-knowing, and omnipresent God could allow so much innocent suffering.

Even though most of my EMDR therapy sessions were difficult to get through, some of them provided glimpses of something spiritual, although I still felt shut off from God. I was still struggling with God's silence, or maybe I was just so angry with God that I was turned off at the notion of anything having to do with a God. In other words, therapy helped heal my relationship with myself and with Jacob's memory, but my relationship with God had not improved.

4

A FATHER'S
FAITH

When Brea and I told our daughters that Jacob had died, I could tell they were going into shock. They didn't cry or show much emotion at all.

At their age, the finality of death was incomprehensible. To them, it was as if he had gone on a trip and at some point would come back.

In retrospect, their lack of emotion did seem strange to us. Not long before this, several chickens we were raising had wandered into our back yard and were killed by our dogs. All of the kids were upset. The girls screamed at the top of their lungs and shrieked in terror at the sight of their chickens, dead. Now their brother had died, and they showed none of the same emotion.

When we talked to Paula, our therapist, about

the way they reacted to Jacob's death, she explained that in that moment, and for many months going forward, their young brains would protect them from reality and only allow them to handle as much as they could process. She went on to tell us that the most important thing the girls wanted to know was that we were okay and were going to be able to keep them safe. Paula told us that if we were able to figure out a way to be present and available for our daughters to make them feel safe, it would give them a higher probability of grieving well.

But the real question in our minds was whether we could ever again be the parents to them that we used to be.

Almost immediately, both girls started trying to comfort us in their own ways. They sat right next to us and held our hands and asked if we were okay. When we came into the room and our eyes were puffy and teary, they asked us if we had been crying and then gave us a hug. The girls became lifelines for Brea and me. Being next to them physically was one of the few things that gave me any comfort. They provided a ray of light when it felt like darkness was overtaking us. It also reminded us in brief doses that we had daughters who were counting on us to keep going and not give up.

"I Love You with All My Heart"

One day after I got home from visiting Jacob in the cemetery, I walked into our playroom and found Kelsey playing on the floor by herself. I had been crying, hard, and must have looked like hell. I walked over and lay down on the floor next to her. I was at the end of my rope, and I just needed some comfort. I grabbed her little hand and held it and soaked up the moment. She was keeping me alive, and she didn't even know it. This little hand was holding a mountain of grief and pain, and she did it effortlessly. There was something in the touch of her hand that gave me hope and it reminded me why I needed to make it through the rest of the day.

Before I got up from the floor, I told her that I loved her—just like I had a thousand times before. I figured I would get the usual response, "I love you too, Daddy." But instead, she looked at me and paused. In a quiet voice she said, "Daddy, I love you with all my heart." It caught me off guard and I froze. This is what Jacob would say back to Brea and me when we told him that we loved him. I almost didn't believe what I had heard. Suddenly, I felt like I had some interaction in some way with Jacob again—he was helping both of us through the moment saying, "Okay, Daddy, you can do this. You can make it. I love you with all my heart and I'm right here with both of you. I'm holding your hand too. Don't give up on the girls. Don't give up on yourself. I'm here with all of you. We're still all together and I'm going to help you all through this."

Even though both girls were several years older than Jacob, they had loved doting over him and they were all very close. Jacob hadn't gotten to the age when a little brother becomes the pest; not only was he their brother, but he was their playmate and friend. Without Jacob, everything was going to change for the girls. The house was going to be quieter, with their parents grieving, and their family and friends feeling sorry for them. We knew they needed help, and we knew that we had very little to offer them.

The Girls and Their Art

We didn't wait long to get Kendall and Kelsey into counseling. About six weeks after Jacob died, Paula referred us to a wonderful place called the Children's Bereavement Center of San Antonio where children who have lost a sibling or parent are able to get counseling for free. After we talked it through with the girls, we decided to set up a time for all of us to visit together.

On our first visit, we were given a tour of the different therapy rooms they had available for kids. It's a two-story building with a music room, dress-up room, art room, a room to hit things, and other areas for children to express their feelings. Pictures of children, mothers, and fathers are placed on the wall in the stairwell by their loved ones as a way to honor them.

We eventually made our way up to an art room with one of the counselors. She gave each of us a white sheet of paper and then asked us to pick out paint colors that represented the way we felt at that moment. I can remember picking out very dark colors. Black to represent emptiness, gray to represent a feeling of sadness, and red because I was so angry at God, myself, and the entire situation. Next, we put each of our colors in a contraption that spun the colors out onto the paper. We each took a turn and then looked at our pieces of paper together. None of us had any bright happy colors and we all felt like our pieces of paper accurately represented how we felt on the inside. It was one of the first times the girls were verbal and open about the way they were feeling.

Kendall and Kelsey grieved in their own unique ways. One of them was very quiet and didn't like talking at length about anything related to Jacob or how she was feeling. In fact, she didn't talk about Jacob unless she was asked direct questions. We could tell she didn't know how to talk about what was going on and she wasn't comfortable verbalizing her feelings. As her dad, I wanted to be able to help her, but I probably made it worse at times pushing her to talk about it when she wasn't ready.

The other one became easily frustrated by simple things that hadn't bothered her previously. A homework problem or having to pick out the right clothes for the day could send her off the edge, which worried us because it was so uncharacteristic for her. After talking to therapists about it, we realized it was a way of dealing with the new stress and sadness added to her life. We were given reassurance that her behavior was very normal and a healthy way for a child to grieve.

Although the girls were sad and missing Jacob, the emotion they most struggled with was fear: fear for their own safety and for their parents' well-being. The girls were worried about our health because it directly affected their sense of safety. For the first time in their lives, they saw their mom and dad unable to physically and mentally function. They were scared and confused to see us in this state, and they didn't know how long it would last.

After this accident that took away their little

brother, they became aware of the fragility of life and their own mortality. Before, death had only been something they heard people talk about or saw on television. Now they were experiencing the devastation and full spectrum of emotions that come with losing an immediate family member. Like all of us, they were also trying to wrap their minds around the death of a child. I think it deeply affects all human beings because we know at our core that the death of a child goes against the natural order of life.

Both of the girls slept in our bedroom with us for six months after the accident. It made them feel closer to us and safer. Brea and I welcomed this, because we were comforted by being together. This nightly ritual was a good representation of how we were going to hunker down together and lean on each other in our pain. We were all hurting and we were all in this together.

We tried our best to cry only privately because we knew it affected the girls. Sometimes it was impossible to hide it, though. Brea or I could just start crying for no reason while we were sitting at dinner, lying in bed talking, watching a show on television, or listening to a song on the radio. Unfortunately, we never knew when the grief was going to hit us or how long it would last.

And sometimes it wasn't tears, it was anger. If I'd get in a fight with Brea, I'd drive around on back roads, go for a walk, or visit the cemetery. It upset the girls to see me leave in anger. One of their biggest fears was whether Brea and I were going to be alright and if we were going to be around to take care of them, so leaving was a terrible way of handling the situation. It wasn't fair to Brea and it scared the girls and really disrupted our home. Brea confronted me multiple times about it. Finally, I realized how much it was hurting the girls by creating more fear and uncertainty when they were already trying to process overwhelming emotions.

Brea and I also noticed the girls were starting to get irritated that everything in our lives was centered on Jacob.

I got a tattoo of Jacob's initials, our whole family wore bracelets with Jacob's name on them, and we put on an annual fundraiser to honor Jacob. It made sense that they would feel left out. Paula told us it was normal for siblings to get jealous of a sibling that had passed away. She recommended that we learn to talk about the silly things or even some negative things Jacob did instead of only talking about the good things. Grieving parents tend to put their deceased child on a pedestal, glorify them, and make them larger than life. It is so easy for me to do that with Jacob, and I have to consciously make an effort not to.

WILL THEY EVER PRAY AGAIN? WILL I?

Before Jacob's accident, we routinely sat down for dinner as a family and prayed before our meal. Either Brea or I would pray, and sometimes even Jacob would say a little prayer. Jacob's prayer was usually very short and sweet: "Thank you, God. Amen." That was it, and that was enough.

After Jacob died, sitting down and starting a meal became awkward. We'd sit there and look at each other, wondering who was going to pray. I had no intention of praying because I didn't know what to pray for and didn't know if prayer would do any good. I'm not one to fake it if I don't believe in something. Brea looked over at me, communicating without saying a word. In a matter of two seconds our eyes had the following conversation:

Brea: "Are you going to pray?"

Me: "No. We've talked about this already a hundred times. I don't want to. I understand it's weird for the girls. But, I'm so pissed at God, I don't even want to pretend I'm praying."

Brea: "Okay, okay. I get it. Alright, I'll do it."

Brea: "By the way, I know you're angry with God, but it's all over your face. Could you chill out a little and put a smile on your face?"

Me: "Sure. But, I'm not going to like it."

Brea: "Thank you. I love you."

Me: "I love you too. Could you please say your prayer now so we can eat?"

With my trust in God waning, I was worried that my actions and words about faith would affect the girls. Brea had some concerns, as well, about how my increasing doubts were going to affect them. On multiple occasions she said she wanted the two of us to agree on what we would and wouldn't talk to the girls about with regard to God, because we no longer saw eye to eye on some pretty foundational theological questions. I had become open to different understandings of God that she wasn't comfortable with, and she didn't want me to say something that might confuse our children.

In the past, I had been on a number of Christian retreats where the subject of being the spiritual head of the household was discussed and studied at length. I thought it was very important that I helped to make sure our home was a place where our children learned about God. I was intent on teaching my children how to pray and praying for them. And, I made sure that I was leading my family with Christian values and principles, hoping to pass down a faith tradition they would have for the rest of their life. I had become pretty good in my role as spiritual head of the household. But now, I didn't feel like I even knew where to start with God. How was I going to pray with my family anymore, when I hadn't a clue what to pray for? My anger at God had pretty much shut down my desire to pray. And when I did pray, it wasn't a pleasant experience because my prayers had turned into screaming at God.

When the girls could see that I had lost interest in wanting to go to church, they started feeding off of it. Suddenly, they didn't want to go either.

Growing up in church was a very positive experience for me, so I didn't want my personal feelings and struggles to turn church into a negative experience for my children. But on Sunday mornings, Brea and I debated about whether we were going to go to church. I'd say that it was a waste of time because we were going to hear another sermon I didn't agree with, and I knew we would both end up leaving unsatisfied and disheartened. She told me that we needed to go for the girl's sake, and at minimum she wanted to go to listen to the music.

There was nothing bad about our pastor's sermons in particular, even though his theology was a bit different than mine. But the truth is, in our suffering and pain no church or preacher could have satisfied our longing for solidarity. I was going to be upset with any sermon that talked about the goodness of God or the love of God because I was so angry with what I thought God had done to Jacob and our family.

Even though I sat in protest with my arms folded in the pew, pouting like a toddler, I agreed to go to church because I knew Brea was right. It was important that we show our girls that we weren't giving up on our faith even though it was difficult. I realized that my daughters' faith would have to be their own. Of course, we have some influence on our children's spiritual lives, but children grow up. Many lifelong evangelicals I know left church when they entered college even though they'd been immersed in Christianity growing up. No matter how hard we try to teach our children about God, they have to find their own faith and beliefs. Otherwise, their spiritual lives will lack depth and meaning.

Brea and I are perfect examples of this. She didn't grow up regularly attending church or being deeply immersed in church culture. When we started dating, she started going to church with me, and her faith only grew from that point on. Since Jacob passed away, her faith has sustained her and hardly wavered at all. She would tell you that her relationship with God has only grown stronger over the last few years.

My experience has been much different. My parents did everything they could to make sure I grew up in a home where Jesus was lifted up as a model and faith was central to life. That being said, the faith I had built and had leaned on growing up was not necessarily one that had been tested or one that I had much ownership in.

Then, when I needed it most, my faith crumbled.

I hope that my daughters don't ever experience the same type of pain we have. They will certainly have struggles. But, when they face hard times, I want them to lean on their faith and find God to be a sanctuary. However, they may not.

After discussing our issues at length in therapy together and by working through tense conversations, Brea and I learned a number of lessons to help us walk our daughters through their own faith journey while we both still wrestle with faith and spirituality after Jacob's death. Although we aren't going to compromise our own beliefs, we aren't going to try and force beliefs or theology on our children out of fear. As parents we have to exercise another type of faith—faith that our own children will make good decisions and find their own faith.

As much as we would like to force our children to believe and act a certain way, it's just not possible. A forced faith is not an authentic faith.

LEANING ON MY DAUGHTER'S FAITH

Kelsey had heard stories of Jesus coming back to earth from the Revelation story. She would say on multiple occasions that she was ready, so all of our family could be together again. Her hope in Jesus's return gave her peace.

I envy faith like Kelsey's and Brea's.

I long for a relationship and trust in God like they have. They live with a peace I've never had. Even though I've trusted God in the past, I didn't trust like they do now. I was never all in. Doubting and questioning is in my DNA. I'm an analyzer by nature and by trade. I guess you could say that's the way God made me. I just wish believing were easier. I still don't pray out loud with the girls like I used to. I'm not vocal about God, like before. I want to be a father who prays with his kids and I want to encourage them in their faith because I see the hope, values, and meaning that belief in God can add to life.

Since I'm still working on repairing and

rebuilding my own faith and have so many questions, I'd be disingenuous if I pretended to have something I don't. I'm unsure of so much, that I don't feel confident talking about God, the Bible, or my theological commitments. My hesitation is centered around trust. Ever since I was a kid, my faith was built on a God I trusted to act a certain way. When God seemed to operate outside of my expectations, then I lost my trust in him.

Before the accident as I walked through the house and kissed each of our children on the forehead and prayed a short prayer over them, I trusted God to keep them safe. But God did not keep Jacob safe.

I no longer know how to pray or what to pray for. I'm stuck. It makes me feel like I'm less of a father, like a Christian man who doesn't make the mark. There were so many "right" things I used to do that made me look like a good example of a Christian husband and father. Now, I feel like I'm not doing enough or that my kids and wife aren't getting what they deserve.

My hope is that God finds me. Lord knows, I've been looking for him.

We now talk openly and candidly about spiritual questions and doubts in our home. We have all talked together about my anger with God and how that may have changed how I think about or relate with God.

Our hope is that in sharing our struggles with the girls and being open and honest, they will always feel free to share with us the struggles or questions they may have.

Over the last five years I have labored to imagine our family being happy. I didn't know what it was going to look like to move forward as just the four of us. Mostly, I didn't want to face that reality, so I fought against it as long as I could. As time and therapy healed us, we could laugh together again. We were able to enjoy those moments even though Jacob wasn't with us. The pain and grief were still right under the surface, but we learned to enjoy each other again, and together we figured out how to make our family experiences joyful again.

In the summer of 2015, we decided to go on a trip to Los Angeles together for a short vacation. We had never been to California before and we were ready to escape the Texas heat. On the itinerary was a trip to Disneyland, a concert, and some days spent relaxing on the beach. One of the first things we did was rent bikes and ride down the boardwalk together. The weather was perfect, and we were staying right on the beach in Malibu. One day we decided to go down to the beach and let the girls play. We had to walk a few hundred yards to the water from our hotel. We set up a spot underneath a big umbrella. With the sun beaming, we were in heaven. The girls went down to the water's edge and let the waves come up to their ankles. They squealed at how cold it was and ran out. We all laughed and tried to see how deep we could bear the cold water climbing up our legs.

Brea and I decided to sit back down and warm up in the sun. As we watched the girls, Brea and I reflected on how happy the girls seemed to be. They had both come a long way. We felt so much joy seeing them run in the water and play with each other. They had been through more pain and heartache than many adults will ever experience. They had experienced the trauma of seeing their parents at the lowest points of their lives. They had witnessed their parents performing CPR on their little brother, screaming at God to save him.

If you had seen them and didn't know their story that day on the beach, you would have thought nothing of it. Yes, they had experienced tragedy, but they were healing and had become stronger than before. In that moment I realized that even though we would still live with pain and sadness, we were going to be okay. We are a family of five with one of us missing, but the four of us remaining here were going to love each other and hold each other as best we could.

During one of Kendall and Kelsey's final therapy sessions at the Bereavement Center, the person leading their group told the girls to pick out one of the rooms to go demonstrate how they were feeling. Brea was with them while they went up together into a room full of figurines. When the girls finished setting up the figurines they wanted, Brea noticed something about all of them. Each of them represented something about Jacob. There were superheroes, toy trucks, soldiers, and cowboys.

Brea and I wonder if the girls will remember Jacob, or if they will forget him. Honestly, it's one of those things I worry about. Even though they only spent three years with Jacob, he was a very large part of their everyday lives and they loved him so much. They may not fully remember all of that, but we do.

That final therapy session showed us that they do think about him and that he is an important person in their lives, even though they may not talk about him.

I'm incredibly proud of Kendall and Kelsey and the young ladies they are turning out to be. The pain and suffering they have endured at such a young age will only make them that much stronger, more compassionate, and loving women. Their little brother dying was *a* defining moment in their lives, but it will not define who they are for the rest of their lives.

5

WILL OUR MARRIAGE SURVIVE?

The week following Jacob's death was a blur. One of the more vivid and defining moments that week happened when I walked into our bedroom and found Brea crying in the corner. It is still gut wrenching when I think of it. It's the most desperate I've seen her. We had both been crying off and on all day, but this was different.

When I sat down next to her she said, "I just want to die. My baby, I can't live without him. I don't want to do this."

Brea had always been the person who lifted me up, gave me hope, and kept me going when things got bad. I had looked to her for encouragement and help for the last twenty years, and now we were both crumpled up on the floor, overcome with hopelessness, and ready to give up. I was at the lowest point in my life. What was I going to do if the person I relied on the most didn't think there was a reason to go on either?

Brea is naturally optimistic. She is the positive person in our marriage. She sees the good in nearly everything and everyone. I'm naturally cynical and I have always had to be intentional in order to be grateful. So seeing Brea at her lowest completely freaked me out. Brea's a fighter—I've never seen her give up on anything, and I'd never heard anything that resembled hopelessness from her. But this experience was so much more profoundly painful and difficult than anything she had faced before.

All I could think to do was lie down next to her and cry with her. I begged her to stop saying that she didn't want to live. I couldn't imagine having to live without her too, and I couldn't handle hearing those words coming out of her mouth. We had always been each other's biggest supporters, holding each other up when we needed it. Now, we were two parents lying together on the floor of our bedroom, heartbroken, sobbing uncontrollably, and losing hope, in total despair.

I had no idea how we were going to survive as

parents who had lost a child. But, I don't think either one of us could have predicted how it was going to affect our marriage.

I CAN'T FIX THIS

For most of my life, I've operated under the assumption that all problems have solutions: I see a problem, I analyze it, and I fix it. But the events of June 12 led to disastrous consequences for which there were no solutions. There was nothing I could do to bring Jacob back or to right what I felt I had done wrong. Even so, I went into fix-it mode and frantically tried to think of ways to do something, anything, to make things better, to fix Brea's grief.

The first solution was to give Brea another baby.

Neither of us felt like we were done raising kids or toddlers. After being around other bereaved parents, we found out this is common. It was easy to think that the excitement, joy, and new love for a baby will bring welcome relief from the pain, sadness, and darkness we were living in. Even though we weren't consciously trying to replace Jacob, there was something inside us that believed that another child would ease our despair.

But in reality, all we really wanted was the child we didn't have anymore.

Even if we did decide to try and have another baby, it was going to be very difficult for us. When Jacob was born, Brea had her third C-section. We decided beforehand to have Brea's tubes tied during the procedure. We had two girls and now a boy, so we felt like our family was complete. I didn't want Brea to undergo unnecessary risks, so having her tubes tied made perfect sense at the time. Looking back, we both regret that decision.

A few days after Jacob died, I spoke privately with my sister about whether it's possible for a woman to have kids after having her tubes tied. Without making me feel like an idiot, my sister gently suggested that it might be too early for that conversation. Eventually, Brea and I did talk through the possibility of having another baby. We went back and forth between wanting to do it and feeling like we shouldn't. We talked to family members about the idea. Everyone was supportive of whatever decision we made and no one objected to us trying to have another baby. For the most part, I think people wanted us to find some meaning again, and if it was in having another baby, then we should go for it.

Within a few months, Brea met with her gynecologist to discuss the risks of having another C-section, since those risks are what made us decide to have the tubal ligation in the first place. The doctor evaluated her, examined how her previous incisions had healed, and discussed the risks involved. She told Brea that the risks were low enough and if we wanted to try, she could have a fourth C-section.

After she got the go-ahead from the gynecologist, we met with a fertility doctor to talk through our options and the tubal reversal procedure. We learned it would be quite a process, and we were committed to doing it in hopes of getting pregnant. One of the major steps was the actual reversal, which is done via laparoscopic surgery. It's supposed to be a fairly routine surgery lasting around two hours. We decided to go ahead with the procedure.

ANOTHER BABY

After five hours of surgery, the doctor told me that Brea was fine and in recovery. He went on to say that there had been a slight complication during surgery, which is why it had taken so long.

I was totally relieved that the issues she had weren't major and she was recovering comfortably. I couldn't wait to go back and see her. To our amazement, within a month Brea was pregnant. A little over a year after Jacob's accident, we were expecting another child, and we were thrilled. It brought a little more hope into all of our lives, and it felt like there was something new for all of our family to look forward to.

The week after we found out she was pregnant we went on a vacation with our extended family, and there we told them all about the pregnancy. They were thrilled. But Brea started spotting on the first night of the vacation, and she drove herself to urgent care to get checked out, just to be safe. Two hours later she called me, sobbing. She'd miscarried. We had lost another child.

Immediately, I got terribly angry at God again. As if we hadn't been through enough, now we had more grief to contend with. To be frank, my anger didn't last long. It turned into indifference. Either God had abandoned us, wasn't who I thought he was, or wasn't there at all. I was too exhausted to try and figure it out any longer.

Brea and I had put so much hope into this new baby. We talked about it and dreamed about it. The new child had lifted our spirits and occupied our minds, and the disappointment of the miscarriage was crushing. Now more than ever, I was wondering what use God was at all. What use was having any faith? Even at the deepest, darkest time, when we prayed for God to do something good, it failed. None of it made any difference.

Some weeks after the miscarriage, Brea had more tests run and they found that both tube openings had closed up, not letting the fertilized egg pass through the fallopian tubes properly. We had one final option available to us: in vitro fertilization, which is expensive, time consuming, and intense for the mother. Brea needed to have several procedures done and then take a regimen of drugs to increase the probability of a successful pregnancy. Again, Brea and I talked with our therapist and family members. In the end, we decided that as long as we had the money to try, we would go through the effort to make it happen.

After several meetings with the doctor, the next step for Brea was to start taking the medications and shots before the actual procedure would take place. To make it worse, she would have to give herself shots in the stomach. I walked into the bathroom with Brea when she was supposed to give herself her first shot. She was crying and said she didn't think she could do it.

In that moment, the full weight of all that we were trying to do overwhelmed us. We were still grieving, trying to care for our young daughters, dealing with the miscarriage, working on our marriage, trying to get pregnant—it was too much to bear.

That day we decided to not go through with IVF. We had pushed ourselves to our limit, and it was time to stop. We were not yet healed. We were trying too hard to run away from Jacob's death. The thought of another baby had become something to keep our minds busy and allowed us to feel hope again. The costs of feeling hope, though, had become too much for us to handle. So we stopped. We had to let go of the dream we had of having another child.

WILL YOU FORGIVE ME?

Brea and I basically grew up together, and over the course of twenty years we had formed patterns of relating. She's the positive one, and I'm more pessimistic. And I have long leaned on her to pick me up when I'm feeling low. But grief threw a wrench in our well-worn patterns, and we started to frustrate one another. Brea cried in quiet moments throughout the day, keeping to herself. I wailed on the floor for thirty minutes at a time, and I expected her to help me feel better. I had always been somewhat co-dependent with her, and this trauma magnified the problem.

We talked with Paula about the difficulty we were having and that we were frightened that it would put a wedge between us. It strained our relationship, and we'd heard rumors of high divorce rates among grieving parents. The last thing either of us needed or wanted was to be at odds with each other. We didn't want the relationship we had built over decades to be destroyed by something neither one of us had any control over. Paula told us that all people experience grief differently. The important thing to remember was that we were individuals first, not a couple. And the only way we were going to save our marriage was to first take care of ourselves. Airline flight attendants always tell you to put your mask on first and then help your child, because you can't help them if you don't make sure you survive first. The most important thing, she told us, was that we needed to let the other person grieve in whatever way they wanted as long as they didn't hurt themselves.

One example of a bad pattern is that the first year after Jacob's accident, I fell into an unhealthy routine of seeking something from Brea that she could not give me. While I was at work, I would think about Jacob or see a picture of him, and it triggered all sorts of negative emotions. I'd spiral into an emotional mess, then I'd pick up my phone and text Brea, telling her how sorry I was and that I wished that I could change everything.

I did this dozens of times to her over the first year. For a little while she responded and told me the same thing she had told me face-to-face countless times before: she didn't blame me, and she knew that I was sorry. Still, part of me didn't believe her. I was sure she blamed me, at least a bit, and I hounded her to admit it. She told me there was no reason to tell her I was sorry, but I couldn't stop. I convinced myself that I was doing this for her. But, subconsciously I was stuck in co-dependent behavior. The only way I could properly manage my guilt was by dealing with it personally. I had to find a way to be at peace with my responsibility for Jacob's death. No one else was going to be able to help me.

Our co-dependent relationship had worked for us in the past, but it wasn't going to work with an issue this big. Paula told Brea to quit taking the bait when I put it out there. Ultimately, Brea realized she needed to not say anything at all when I'd tell her I was sorry.

Paula warned her that it might make me mad, and it did. Brea's non-response left me with nowhere to go but to sit with myself. And I didn't like my own company very much. It took some time and a number of arguments for us to work through it, but eventually I realized there wasn't anything Brea was going to do or say that could help me feel less guilty.

Unequally Yoked

Initially, Brea and I both leaned heavily on our faith to help us get through the days and weeks after the accident. We both prayed harder than we ever had before, spending our mornings journaling, praying, or looking up Bible verses to find comfort. Neither one of us understood how God could have let this happen to Jacob, but we didn't waver in our trust that God would get us through this.

For months we were on the same page, but then I started getting more and more unsettled with the lack of answers or understanding I found in the Bible and through prayer. While Brea felt comforted and strengthened by God, I felt like God was further and further away. For the first time in our marriage, we were going in different directions spiritually. While I became angrier with God, she embraced her faith. She prayed harder, she journaled more, and she trusted more. I couldn't—and it wasn't for lack of trying. I wanted to feel God's presence and to find rest from my search for answers. Brea found what she was looking for, but I ran into one dead end after another.

Any sentence that included the phrase "God has a plan..." would instantly put me into defense mode. "Do you really believe it was God's plan for my son to die the way he did?" I argued back. For most Christians I knew, the idea that God has a plan for everything is acceptable and comforting when unfortunate life events happen. It's almost always possible to find a positive outcome or a silver lining. This type of thinking works fine when it's not a life-and-death situation. I might be able to go along with God having a plan for me to lose a job. But, it is much more difficult to ascribe intentionality to God when it's life or death.

If God is in total control of all things, then rape, murder, and torture are all events that God has put in motion. On the other hand, if God is not in control of those events, are we to view God as a powerless, inactive bystander?

Let me say this unequivocally: Nothing good comes from the death of a child. Period.

As a grieving parent, I can search for meaning in my life and perhaps even find meaning *in* my pain. In fact, finding meaning in life is what kept me alive in my worst circumstances. But I reject the idea that God wants or plans for something so horrific to happen to children.

To those who believe God has a plan for

everything, as Jacob's father I ask, "What about God's plan for Jacob?" Don't tell me that Jacob is better off not having lived a full life because he is in heaven already. If you actually believe that, why don't we all commit suicide or let our children die from illnesses? When we take this type of statement to its logical conclusion, this is where we end up.

I can't believe God only planned for Jacob to live here for three years and it was "his time." God created this little boy to live with a family who loves him, a boy full of adventure, curiosity, and spark. For God then to orchestrate, or at least allow, Jacob's death alone in a hot car, scared and in pain, seems absolutely ridiculous and nonsensical.

A true statement about God should have given us peace. I certainly prayed for peace and understanding around this type of theology, but it never came. The truth may hurt, but when you hear it you feel it in your bones. You know it to be true even if you don't like it.

When I discussed my questions about God's action or inaction with Brea, it quickly devolved into an argument, tears, or both. We didn't disagree on everything, but I didn't understand why she didn't feel exactly the same why I did. I envied her strong faith and spirituality. My constant questioning and talking to her about my anger at God became frustrating and painful for Brea to hear. I pushed her on her faithfulness to the beliefs about God that I thought were wrong. I didn't understand why she was okay with some things in light of what we had experienced. This was the first time we had real differences in what we believed.

"Do not be unequally yoked" was something we had taken very seriously our entire marriage. "Do not be yoked together with unbelievers. For what do righteousness and wickedness have in common? Or what fellowship can light have with darkness?" (2 Corinthians 6:14). That's a verse we had heard a lot, used in many teachings and sermons to teach the importance of surrounding yourself with other Christians. It was even more important never to marry someone who was not Christian. There was no way a marriage could work if both weren't Christians and they both didn't have deep trust in God. That's what we'd been taught, and that's what we believed.

Brea and I had always agreed on almost all facets of our faith. In many ways, our faith was not individual. Our spirituality was so much a part of who we were as a couple that it didn't seem right for us to have different beliefs about certain things. Actually, I would have thought something was wrong with our marriage if we had differing beliefs.

So this was uncharted territory for us. We both questioned what it meant for us as a couple. Neither one of us was the same person after Jacob died. The man Brea married was a good Christian. I said the right things, did the right things, and believed the right things. Now, Brea had to figure out how to be married to a man whose faith had crumbled.

We've worked hard over the last five years, and we've taken nothing in our marriage for granted. To get to a place where we could find common ground took countless hours of counseling, long and difficult conversations, and a heavy dose of intention on both of our parts. We had several breakthroughs that helped us move forward despite not being "equally yoked."

First, we realized that we are primarily individuals. We had to embrace the fact that our spirituality comes from within ourselves. This forced us to dive deeper into how we think about the world and what we think about God than we ever had before. Rediscovering ourselves as individuals has actually made us stronger as a married couple.

And we've discovered that it's not the end of the world as a Christian couple if we don't have the same theological views. I don't have to try and convince her of something and she doesn't feel the pressure to convince me. We're both on a journey. We accept and love one another for who we are as complete people, and that love is not hinged on how well we are following the Christian couple rulebook.

MARRIAGE

As we were driving back home from an out-of-town visit with my family on a Sunday evening, I tried to hold it together to keep the tears that were welling up in my eyes from blurring my vision as the sun set. It had only been a few months since Jacob had died, and I was missing him desperately. Those first few car rides without him were unbearable—the car was noticeably quieter and there was an empty space where he used to be.

As we entered our driveway, tears streamed down my face. I got out of the car as fast as I could in order to keep my daughters from seeing me and having to explain why I was crying again. I went straight into our bathroom to get my hair clippers. Then I went and got my Bible and an extension cord. I snuck back outside. By now it was dark and the only way I could see was by the light of my phone. I set my Bible down on the driveway, plugged in my hair clippers, and did the only logical thing someone feeling hopelessly sad and losing their mind would do: I started shaving my head.

If I was going crazy, this was a pretty good start. Had the neighbors seen me, I'm sure they would have called 911. A grown man, lying down on the driveway in the dark, sobbing and shaving his head.

Just months before Jacob's accident I had started cutting his hair with these clippers. Brea didn't like it much because it made him look older, and I cut his little wavy red hair too short. But cutting Jacob's hair was a way I felt closer to him. And now I wanted to cut my hair like his.

When I finished shaving my head, my next impulse was to start yelling at God and reading Bible verses out loud. I went on my usual rant, asking for God to speak to me: "God, can you see how much I need you now? Where are you? How am I going to make it?"

After looking for me all over the house, Brea opened the door, walked outside, and quietly called my name. "Jason?"

"Yeah—I'm over here," I said in a garbled tone.

She asked, "What are you doing?"

"I don't know."

She walked over to me and must have been a little freaked out by the state she found me in. I wouldn't have blamed her if she had been angry with me or scared. Instead, what she did do was a defining moment in our marriage. She walked over and sat down next to me. She pulled me over close to her and laid my head in her lap. And she started rubbing her fingers through my newly chopped hair and let me cry like a baby.

She didn't tell me I was crazy or yell at me for cutting all of my hair. She didn't try to fix me. She was quiet. She just sat with me. (She did giggle a little at how ridiculous I looked.)

Eventually, every marriage is tested to some degree. Maybe through financial troubles, infidelity, loss of a job, a spouse who is checked out, emotional issues due to childhood trauma, or health problems. The friction and stress brought on by these experiences can lead us to question how we're going to hold our marriage together.

If we hadn't already been in therapy, I'm not sure how Brea would have reacted to the state she found me in. In our sessions we were able to talk through our difficulties, our pain, and our disagreements. We were given tools and insights we could use to help us navigate the strains being put on our relationship.

Brea could have reacted differently that night. She could have turned around and walked off. She could have yelled at me and started crying. But she didn't. She chose to love and hold on to the broken man who was different in many ways from the one she married. We've said many times that we have walked through hell together. Our marriage could have easily been torn apart by the death of our son. But instead I know that our marriage is much stronger than it was before, and we have been given some amazing tools to guide us. One thing is for sure: whatever inevitable difficulty we face in the future, we'll be doing it together.

6

GOD

Jacob is buried in a cemetery just a few miles from
our house. When we picked out a casket and talked
about the funeral service with the funeral home,
they asked us where he would be buried. We had
no idea. There was a cemetery on a road we drove
up and down every day. We could have buried Jacob
there, but we figured it would be too hard to pass his
grave every day and be brought face-to-face with our
grief. Each time we passed, we would feel the need to
visit him, or guilty if we didn't.

There was a pretty Catholic cemetery we knew
about. We inquired with the church, but they
wouldn't let us buy a plot there because we didn't
belong to the Catholic Church. We also asked about
a Lutheran cemetery, and we got the same answer.
We kept asking around, and someone told us about
an old cemetery off a back road that wasn't far from

our house, the Post Oak Cemetery. The road to the cemetery is mostly farmland with some houses scattered on large lots. On the approach are two very large post oak trees, probably five or six feet in diameter and forty feet tall. The branches are covered with leaves and sprawl out in massive circumference. The cemetery is enclosed by a simple chain-link fence and gate.

The dark, weathered headstones show that it's an old cemetery with a lot of history. A historical marker in the front gives the history of the cemetery: the first person buried there was a ten-year-old boy in the late 1800s.

A few months after Jacob died, I decided to visit his grave so that I could unload and cry. My grief and sadness had built up to a point that I needed to release it all in a planned and organized way. I had learned that when I felt the urge, I needed to go let it out in a time and place that allowed me to be vocal and open with my emotions. One of those places was the cemetery.

I grabbed a towel out of the back of my truck to sit on, and I walked through the gate toward Jacob's grave. I noticed the new graves, marked by fresh dirt and dying flowers. As a ritual, I looked to see how old the person was when they died. Normally, they were in their seventies or eighties and I'd think,

"Well, at least they had a full life." Those families grieve, too, but I can't help but compare Jacob's short life to the long lives of others. It seems so unfair that Jacob missed so many experiences.

At Jacob's grave, there are rocks painted by kids, and toys from other children. There's a little ceramic cardinal and some seasonal artificial flowers. On the headstone is a picture of Jacob, his birthdate and death date, and a verse from Luke 1:14–15: "He will be a joy and a delight to all those he meets. . . ." At the bottom it says, "We love you to infinity and beyond," borrowed from Buzz Lightyear in *Toy Story*. Jacob was buried in his favorite Buzz Lightyear year T-shirt, shorts, and the cowboy boots he always wore.

I sat down on the towel just in front of his grave, pulled out my phone, and opened it up to the picture roll of him; I have about five hundred pictures of Jacob on my phone. I looked through photos from the last year of his life. There are pictures of him from the summer of 2010, pictures of him on our family river trip, the fall pumpkin patch, our last Christmas together, his third birthday, one of my favorite pictures of him and me at Kendall's track practice, and one of the last pictures of him and the girls, on a shopping trip the weekend before the accident.

As I scrolled through the pictures, I started to cry

uncontrollably. The more I looked at him the harder it got, but the tears came easier and easier.

Then I started asking God one question after another:

"Why? Why did you let this happen?"

"Why would you do this to our family?"

"How can this be what you wanted?"

"What did we do to deserve this?"

"Why don't you help me?"

"Today I want answers! Just tell me you are here. Please give me a sign that you are in control of this and that you are here with me. Do something. Speak to me. If you've done it before with others, why won't you show yourself to a grieving parent? I'll tell the world about you if you make it that easy. Why wouldn't you want to make it that easy?"

I was crying so hard that I could barely catch my breath, and I was yelling these questions at God hoping for answers. They were questions I'd asked a thousand times, but I asked them—I shouted and screamed and cried them—with an intensity I never had before.

I begged and pleaded with God to show me something. But, God did not do anything. God did not give me a miracle. I didn't hear anything. I didn't see anything.

I felt abandoned by God. The God who says,

"Come to me all who are weary and burdened and I will give you rest," wasn't offering me any comfort.

This was the first time I started to consider that God might not exist at all. If God did exist, and if God loved me, then I wouldn't feel so empty and distant from God. After all, I was seeking and running toward God. I was doing everything I could to find him. I prayed, I read my Bible, I asked questions, and I didn't get anything.

Maybe everything I ever thought about God was wrong.

Maybe there is no God.

I Thought We Had a Deal

I would describe my relationship with God growing up as a fear-based and transaction-oriented relationship. When I did something wrong, I felt like God didn't like me, and in order to regain my good standing, I had to ask for forgiveness. I felt a lot of shame when I did something wrong. Because of my sin, I thought God was disappointed in me and turned his back on me until I repented. This way of thinking was typical in the evangelical circles I grew up in. I was taught that my sin was so bad and God was so holy that he couldn't look at me or hear me unless I asked for forgiveness and was saved by Jesus.

I had to do something in order for God to want to have anything to do with me. In my mind, there were conditions on God's love for me, even though I'd always heard that God loved me. Hearing that God loved me so much that he killed his own child for me was overwhelming in one sense, and also quite terrifying. If God was willing to take out his own son for me, how easy would it be for God to inflict harm or pain on me for any reason at all? If anything, the story of Jesus's crucifixion instilled more fear of God than love or devotion. And the devotion I had in following God was motivated by appeasing God in order to have a "blessed" life.

When I wanted something, I would pray for God to give it to me. As long as I was behaving myself, I figured God would give it to me. Help me get good grades, make my life as easy as possible, help me score this touchdown, help my team win. These things were important to me growing up. And since I had been fairly successful in most things that I did, I figured God was hearing my prayers and was on my side. I also prayed for people to be safe, to keep them from harm, and to heal people that I knew were sick. I'd lived a relatively easy life into my thirties. I felt safe and loved. I witnessed tragedies in other families, but for the most part these were explained by simple statements like, "It must have been God's plan," "God needed another angel," or when things made absolutely no sense at all, "God's ways are not our ways." None of this thinking was tested in my life, but it seemed to work for me so I just went along with it.

My freshman year of college, I took a philosophy class and for the first time encountered an outright atheist who questioned God's existence. I'd lived in a bubble of believers for eighteen years, and when I heard someone question everything I believed in it unexpectedly set me back on my heels. Listening to my philosophy professor was like hearing for the first time that Santa Claus wasn't real. Nonetheless, I kept my faith as best I could. In the back of my mind, I was skeptical of some of the things I'd learned about God's love and providence, but my faith was still working fairly well for me, so why rock the boat?

After college, I got the job I wanted and the wife I wanted, and we started the family we wanted. Life was going better than I could have imagined. I was heavily involved in our church in Corpus Christi, Texas and on the board of a couple of Christian ministries. I was doing all the right things a good Christian man should be doing. I didn't drink too much, I had a good marriage, and I harbored no real vices to speak of. It felt like God and I were on the right track.

When Jacob died, it felt like I had been tricked. I had prayed over our kids to be safe their whole lives. Why didn't God keep Jacob safe? Did I do something that God wanted to punish me for? I had been living a good life, but where was God when I needed him most?

In addition to the prayers asking how God could let this happen, I prayed to God for the strength to get through it. Most of all, I wanted God to give me some sign that Jacob was okay and that God was in control. I felt empty and alone in a way I never expected. Maybe God would whisper to me in an audible voice. Or God would give me a sign that he was near. But God didn't. I felt abandoned. I didn't understand why God wouldn't show me his presence if he were really there. Up to this point, if I prayed to God to fix something or for help, it seemed like God showed up. But now all that was crumbling.

Previously, if something bad happened to me, it was fairly easy to come up with reasons why. The cause was either easily observable, or it must have been God's plan. I always believed there was some higher purpose and good that would come from the circumstance.

But now I searched in vain for an answer as to why God would let Jacob die.

Based on my beliefs, God must have let him die

or allowed this to happen because God was ultimately in control. It made no sense that God would let Jacob die, especially in the manner in which he did. I always believed there was some purpose for the pain in our lives. I heard that notion reinforced on Sunday mornings. Now I wondered: Is there really purpose for all the pain we experience? I used to be able to justify any difficult circumstance by finding some good that could eventually come from it. If I heard that someone was diagnosed with a disease and proceeded to find God through it, I would have argued that God must have used the disease to get their attention. God using or causing a disease to bring about a relationship seemed like a logical tradeoff. After all, the person now has a deeper faith because of their disease, which is what God desired. If I heard of a devastating financial loss that literally brought a married couple to their knees, I would have argued that despite their deep pain and struggling, God must be using this to bring them closer to him. It couldn't have been the years of living beyond their means; it had to be God teaching them a lesson in humility and faith.

I believed God was causing and allowing every single event that happened to humanity, so I concluded that God knew what he was doing—

using all pain and suffering to bring about his will, which must ultimately be good.

But when my child died in a senseless accident, my theology did not make sense to me anymore. What good can come from a child dying? He was an innocent three-year-old boy who had never done anything wrong. He hadn't committed some heinous act against humanity or been a menace to society. Yet, he suffered a painful death and the suffering he experienced had no meaning. The pain he experienced gave no benefit to anyone.

This doesn't seem like something a loving God would do.

When I thought of God as the cause of Jacob's death, fear and anger overtook the space in my mind where faith and hope used to reside.

If this is how God works in the world, then God isn't the loving Father I thought I had; God is the monster in my nightmares.

SWIMMING IN UNCERTAINTY

Fight or flight is in our DNA. We are built to reduce risk and survive. I think that drive to survive leads us to want to control our environment and outcomes, and in order to do that, we're always trying to reason about the situations and circumstances we find ourselves in. When things don't go the way we expect, we question how in the world we got to this point, and we make a point to avoid future pain. When my expectations of life and God failed, questions abounded and confusion swallowed up my certainty. I could not make sense of life, especially since my theology included a good, omnipotent God.

At our core, we are creatures that seek meaning. This leads us to seek reason and meaning in the suffering we go through. Everywhere I looked I could not find any answers that gave meaning or reason to why my young son died. One of my deepest desires is for Jacob's life and death to have meaning in this world. So, I was unwilling to settle for the easy answers I was able to live with before his death. The problem is, too often other people were not comfortable with the uncertainty. So instead, they offered well-intended but wrongheaded religious platitudes, statements that are meant to push out uncertainty. Here are some that I heard:

1) "God is good all the time."

Most of the time this phrase is used to attribute a good or positive outcome to God's work. I connected the good things in my life with God's blessing or favor, believing that God was responsible for them. But what about the bad things that happen? If God is in control of everything, should we be giving credit to God for all the bad, evil, and suffering too?

After Jacob died, whenever I heard someone say, "God is good," I'd think to myself, "If you think God is so good, look what he did to my son. Look what he did to my family. God isn't as good as you think."

I couldn't understand how people could believe in God's sovereignty without attributing to God the bad things in life as well as the good. If God is truly sovereign, God cannot be both all good and all powerful with so much evil and suffering in the world.

Although I don't have all the answers, I do believe God is good. In order for me to reconcile God being good, I stopped believing in the total sovereignty of God. I didn't stop believing in God's power, but instead I stopped believing that God desires or needs to control everything in this world. I think that *love* is God's essential nature, not power.

2) "It was God's will."

The week of Jacob's accident, I heard this statement again and again, even from close friends.

When someone said this out loud, I always held my tongue. What I wanted to say was this: "A three-year-old boy needed to suffer and die in a hot car because that's how God wanted to kill him? Let's be frank here: You are saying that God needed to murder my son for some reason. What good reason is worth the suffering of an innocent boy? If God needs to kill someone, couldn't he do it in a little more humane and loving way? Why not take him in his sleep? A God whose will is to murder innocent people or children doesn't seem very loving at all. This is a God to be feared, not revered."

I don't think God wants to inflict pain or suffering on humans. I think it's God's hope that we all live full lives, experiencing his creation and each other. I find no peace or love in a God who needs to use the death of a child to accomplish his will. Honestly, I think it has to hurt God that so much suffering and devastation is attributed to him.

3) "I don't know why God took Jacob."

Inherent in this statement is the belief that God ordained and caused my son to die, that God *took* him. Someone said this to me at our home within a week of Jacob dying. I had a visceral reaction, and I completely shut down. I had no response. Although this person meant well, statements like this only make the person saying them feel better. But to me, it sounded like he was saying that my son was expendable, that God didn't really need Jacob alive, so God took him back.

In my grief, all I want is my son back. I don't care if God wanted it to happen for his purpose. There's no good purpose, as Jacob's father, for him not to be alive. I think this was a tragic accident and was a confluence of a number of random events and circumstances that came together that day. God did not kill Jacob.

4) "He's in a better place."

Brea and I prayed over our children nearly every night. I used to kiss each one of them on the forehead and say a little prayer. I asked God to bless them and to protect them. But God didn't protect Jacob. God didn't bless him with a long life. For those who say, "He is blessed, he's in a better place," I ask, "What, then, is the value of our lives here on earth? If we are all going to be in a better place, then why do we want to keep living at all?" It's ridiculous to me to think that Jacob was supposed to die at three and that our lives without him are better than what they could have been.

Or is the implication that I wasn't a good enough dad, so that Jacob needed to be somewhere better, safer, more comfortable? That's not what my friend meant, I'm sure, but it is implied in the statement.

Assuming Jacob is with Jesus now, he is in a good place. But as Jacob's father, it doesn't make me feel any better or give me any more peace to think he's in any other place than with me. His absence, even if he's in heaven, makes me sad.

5) "God loves you and is here to comfort you."

I asked God countless times to show me that he loved me, or to show me some sign that he was near, or that Jacob was okay. I didn't get any sign or any relief in the midst of that pain. If anything, the silence pushed me even further away from God.

My beliefs at the time led me to feel anger at God rather than love for or from him. I'm still rebuilding my faith and relationship with God. I don't understand how God comforts us, and I still find it hard to trust God, in the traditional sense of that phrase.

6) "God has a plan."

Quite simply, I don't understand a God whose

plan includes the torture of millions of people during the Holocaust, or the rape and murder of young girls, or the painful death of innocent children like my son. Yet, there are many sermons on Sundays that claim "God has a plan" with so much confidence, and with no explanation for all the innocent suffering and evil in the world.

The sovereignty of God is something I'm still very unsettled on and is an area wherein I'm still searching for theological answers.

7) "God's ways are not our ways."

This is the statement used by many who can't think of anything else to say. It still bothers me that God would make it so difficult to understand who God is, especially if we believe God *wants* us to know him. We let God off the hook by doing theological gymnastics—twisting and turning logic in every possible way until we get to the final argument of know-nothingism, the ultimate cop-out.

The beliefs I had before don't work for me anymore. I don't think God changed. The things I believed and thought changed. God is not who I thought God was.

A QUEST FOR ANSWERS

With the number of unanswered questions piling up, and the contradictions between my beliefs and my experiences, I knew I had to seek out a new way of thinking. My beliefs about God and the Bible couldn't exist side-by-side with the way I was feeling inside. So I went on a quest to find answers and I was determined to search for the truth until I was satisfied. The stakes were too high, in my opinion, to leave these questions with half-answers that came up short and provided no rationale for Jacob's death.

As Jacob's dad, I had an obligation to know why this happened to him. It was my responsibility to find a good answer as to why he suffered and died. Because I couldn't find peace out of my own knowledge and understanding, I started asking people I trusted who had more knowledge about the Bible and God than I did. One conversation after another, I left feeling frustrated and without answers.

Going to church and listening to sermons didn't help either. Almost every sermon I heard included the phrases: "God has a plan for you," "It's God's will," or "God loves you." This isn't surprising given how often these themes show up in scripture. Unfortunately, I couldn't get past the obvious contradictions I saw in light of what I was experiencing. I was so angry and confused most Sundays as we left church that I hoped it was the last time I would have to go through it. Driving off, I felt like I didn't fit in anymore because my theology didn't allow me to believe in God's control over our lives.

Brea and I discussed looking for a different church to attend, but when it got down to it we didn't want to leave the relationships behind we had built over the last few years. We didn't want to start over with a new church or lose connection with the people who had supported us when we needed them during the initial months of our grief.

All the people around me believed the same theology that wasn't working for me. In my heart, I felt like there was something off the mark with the answers I got. Additionally, I wanted to hear from people who had suffered yet still maintained a deep faith in God. I wanted people who were honest about the questions they had and talked openly about their doubts, and people who had experienced the same type of deep loss that I had.

Since my religious beliefs had been handed to me at such a young age, I think my beliefs were built on a shaky foundation. I knew what I believed, but none of it had been tested by suffering. I didn't have any ownership of my trust in God because up to this point, trusting God had resulted in a pretty easy life. When I was really tested, it crumbled. Inside, I felt like I had to start over completely and to define what my faith would look like—that is, if I was going to have any faith at all.

As I ran out of people in my network to question, I started doing more reading and research on my own. Surely someone out there had asked these question and come up with acceptable answers, or at least I hoped so.

One of the blogs I had been reading before Jacob's death was by Tony Jones. I didn't know any theologians personally, but because Tony's writing was accessible enough for me to understand, I wondered if he would respond to an email with my questions. I went to his website, found his email address, and figured I had nothing to lose. I fired off an email, knowing the chances of him responding to me were slim.

Deep down, I hoped he would send me a long email with perfect answers for each of my questions so I could get back to having a faith I could live with. That didn't happen, though. Later that same day, I got a reply email from Tony. He said that he didn't feel it was appropriate to answer these questions through email and that he would like to talk to me.

He said to call him, and he provided his cell phone number.

I couldn't believe it! Call him? What was I going to say? I didn't know this guy at all. I wasn't fond of talking about Jacob or my faith to strangers, so I was pretty hesitant to call him at first. Then I thought, "What if he has the answers I'm looking for? I've got to at least try." So, I got over the fear and gave him a call.

I don't remember everything Tony and I talked about over the phone, but a few things do stand out about that call. The first thing that came out of his mouth was, "I'm so sorry." That certainly meant a lot to me since we didn't even know each other. Throughout our talk, I was hoping he would rattle off his answer to the theodicy question and his understanding of God's sovereignty, but he didn't. (Theodicy is the defense of God's goodness and omnipotence in view of the existence of evil.) Instead, Tony just told me how sorry he was and that he didn't have any good answers to my questions.

I have to admit, I was a little disappointed that another person, a theologian no less, didn't have answers. If he didn't have the answers, then who would? Naïvely, I guess I had I always figured theologians had all the answers to any God question you could come up with. But invariably, every time

I asked the "Why?" questions of anyone, no matter their credentials, I kept hitting a dead end.

Even though I didn't realize it at the time, Tony ended up offering me something more meaningful and lasting than answers to my questions. Most people at this point, especially strangers, were not willing to enter our heartache with us. Our darkness was a scary place to be and it was not for the faint of heart. Tony did what a good friend or pastor should do in this situation. He didn't spout off Bible verses and answers. He simply offered his condolences and was willing to sit with me in my pain.

I will never forget what he did for me, and it will always be with me. From that day forward our friendship grew, and he made himself available by phone and email. We have had many exchanges over the course of the last five years. By chance, Tony also led me to the next theologian I decided to contact with my questions.

GOD WITH US

I stumbled upon a podcast that Tony was a part of that included an interview with a German theologian I had never heard of, Jürgen Moltmann. The interview was a panel discussion, and it wasn't terribly interesting to me until one of the panelists asked this theologian a question that sounded like it could have come from me.

One of the panelists, who had lost a child, asked Moltmann where God was when his son died. The theologian went on to tell a story that is taken from the book *Night*, written by Elie Wiesel.[1]

One day, as we returned from work, we saw three gallows, three black ravens, erected on the Appelplatz. Roll call. The SS surrounding us, machine guns aimed at us: the usual ritual. Three prisoners in chains—and, among them, the little pipel, the sad-eyed angel. . . .

The three condemned prisoners together stepped onto the chairs. In unison, the nooses were placed around their necks.

"Long live liberty!" shouted the two men.

But the boy was silent.

"Where is merciful God, where is He?" someone behind me was asking.

At the signal, the three chairs were tipped over.

Total silence in the camp. On the horizon, the sun was setting.

1. Elie Wiesel, *Night*, trans. Marion Wiesel (Bantam Books; Reissue edition, 1982), 61–62.

"Caps off!" screamed the Lagerälteste. His voice quivered. As for the rest of us, we were weeping.

"Cover your heads!"

Then came the march past the victims. The two men were no longer alive. Their tongues were hanging out, swollen and bluish. But the third rope was still moving: the child, too light, was still breathing. . . .

And so he remained for more than half an hour, lingering between life and death, writhing before our eyes. And we were forced to look at him at close range. He was still alive when I passed him. His tongue was still red, his eyes not yet extinguished.

Behind me, I heard the same man asking: "For God's sake, where is God?" And from within me, I heard a voice answer: "Where is He? This is where—hanging here from this gallows. . . ."

A powerful story indeed, with an even more powerful image of God, and definitely not the God I grew up with. Rather, this is a God who is right there feeling the pain and the suffering of humanity.

The notion of a God who was in our pain with us and suffering with us touched something in my bones. It was one of the first things I had heard since Jacob's death that pointed me in a direction that made some sense. If I was going to believe in God, then it couldn't be this monster who set events into motion, allowing or causing pain and suffering. I don't believe God lets a little boy die a slow painful death with a noose around his neck, or that God lets another little boy die of heat exposure in the back of a vehicle. I can't believe that God just sits back and watches horrors happen with ambivalence.

Professor Moltmann and his wife have experienced the death of a child. Their first child passed away at birth, so he knows what it is to be a grieving parent. We connect with those who have experienced the same pain we have. Addicts listen to other addicts. Divorcees connect with other divorcees. We want to know that we aren't alone and that we belong to a group of fellow sufferers.

I had found a fellow sufferer acknowledging the questions and the pain I was feeling, and he actually did answer my *why* question: He said there is no answer.

People who have suffered greatly find peace in a God who is in solidarity with them. We don't find peace in a God who is distant. A God who is intervening to cause or even allow suffering isn't a God we want to believe in, and in that universal feeling must be some truth.

Some say it's arrogant to feel entitled to answers.

Ultimately, if God is seeking relationships, then God is not going to scoff at our misunderstandings and confusion when we feel betrayed or hurt. That's what we all do in our human relationships. We ask each other: "Why are you acting this way?" "What are you doing?" Engaging with God is about relationship, not disrespect. If I didn't believe in God, then I wouldn't care about these answers. But I do. Asking questions has led me to a more authentic relationship with God. It's not totally repaired at this point. And, I can't say that I trust God like many other people do. But, I haven't totally walked away, even though I don't feel like I get much in return.

Moltmann describes something called the self-limitation of God. In the beginning God is all there was. In order for God to have relationship with humans God had to create them. To create them God had to withdraw and self-limit his space in order to provide space for creation. This self-limitation created a distance that seems to limit God's intervention and activity in this world.

Growing up, I had not heard of Jürgen Moltmann. I started looking up his background and ordered one of his more popular books, *The Crucified God*. In many of his articles and interviews he talked of a God who is close to us in our suffering, not a God who is distant and only intervenes from afar in arbitrary ways. He spoke of the love of God, and suggested that God ultimately must suffer with us in order for God to be a God of love.

Tony gave me Professor Moltmann's address, and I sent him a letter in Germany. There were no guarantees because Professor Moltmann is a sought-after speaker and a prolific writer, but I decided it was worth the try.

Below is the letter I wrote to him:

May 8, 2012

Jürgen Moltmann
72070 Tübingen
Germany

Dear Professor Moltmann,

I was introduced to you by listening to the emergent conversation podcast that featured several speaking sessions of yours. Since then, I've read a couple of your books as well. One of your talks focused around the subject of theodicy. This subject has become of great interest to me, arising out of the most tragic event I've ever experienced. My wife and I are bereaved parents.

My 3-year-old son, Jacob, got up from his nap

on Sunday June 12, 2011, and went outside while I was lying down in our bedroom. He got into our family vehicle, and somehow the doors shut. It was extremely hot that day, and he was unable to get out. I did not find him in time. The worst thing that could ever happen to a parent has happened to us. My wife, two daughters, and I are all going to therapy. It has helped to the extent it can, and we are slowly healing. The devastation of that day is haunting. And, the guilt I feel for not hearing him go outside, or for not lying by his side, or all the what-ifs that I could have done to prevent this are almost too much to bear. But, somehow we are able to get up and do what we must to stay alive and to care for each other.

My entire theology has been shattered. I grew up in a southern Baptist setting where God has everything under control, pre-ordains all events, and where God has a "plan" for everyone. It's hard for me to believe any of that anymore. I prayed for protection over my son nearly every night before bed. Was it not enough? Would one more prayer have saved his life? He was an innocent 3-year-old boy who was full of life, joy, and love. Why would God let these things, absolutely senseless things, happen to beautiful children? I could understand it happening to bad or evil individuals. Or, those whose actions caused them to be put into harmful situations. But this is not the case with Jacob.

I am struggling greatly with many ideas, questions, anger, and certainly even the existence of God. I desperately want to find, feel, and hear from the God you know. But all I receive is silence. If my child was hurting and looking for me, I would cross the globe and go through hell to get to them. To hold them, and to let them know I was there. That I loved them with all my being. And, there would be NO doubt that I was there with them. I have begged God for some whisper, a sign, some reassurance that God, the Bible, and Jesus are all real. But, again I get nothing.

So in my continued search I wanted to contact you and pose to you my thoughts and questions, and hope for any response you wish to give. If you don't have the opportunity or time, that is perfectly fine. I will at least have been able to communicate to you that I greatly appreciate your teachings and writing. I have learned a great deal from you over the last year. Thank you.

I have outlined my questions below:

A. How does Jürgen Moltmann "KNOW" there is a God? Have you ever had an actual experience of God? I must know there is God! I want to "know," not just "believe." I'm so tired of the phrase that "you just have to have faith." Pascal's Wager is not good enough for me anymore. There is too much at stake to live based upon such a feeble argument. What is it that gives you the absolute assurance that what you teach and believe is truth?

B. How is there enough proof of the resurrection of Jesus to prove to you that it's true?

C. If God is good and powerful, why would he not save my 3-year-old son?

D. Does God intervene at all in this world?

E. If God does not intervene in this world, then why do we pray? What purpose is there in prayer?

F. If God intervenes sometimes, and not at other times, then how can he be good all the time?

G. If God "allows" things to happen, then his inaction is still an action. Correct? He is not off the hook for not having prevented something from happening to my son.

H. Do you believe there is a literal Satan?

I. Do you believe God has a plan for each of our lives?

J. If there is no specific plan, then how do you reconcile that understanding with verses that seem to state that God does have our days numbered, etc.?

K. What do you believe those who have passed away, such as my son, are literally doing presently? Are they fully aware? Is their soul sleep? Are they aware of our actions here on earth?

L. Do you think I will be able to parent my son on the "new earth," since those years have been taken away?

M. Do you have any practical steps for how I should move forward at this point? How should I find God? How can I know he is there? How should I pray? How should I study the Bible? I don't know how to move forward with God. I really want to know he is there. That he loves me. And, that I will see my son again.

Thank you for taking the time to read this letter. Any response is greatly appreciated.

Sincerely,
Jason Jones

Looking back, I can see and feel the desperation in my letter. There was so much at stake for me. At the time, my mind was a mess of grief, fear, and frantic desperation. All I wanted to do was find a way to make sense of how this could happen to Jacob and my family, of how God could allow such suffering and pain.

I figured there was very little chance Professor Moltmann would write back. But a couple of weeks later I received a priority letter back from Tübingen. On it was my name and address typed by what looked like an old typewriter. The return address was Jürgen Moltmann.

I couldn't believe it! I ripped open the letter hoping to read the answers I hadn't been able to find up to this point.

Here is the letter I received, reprinted with Professor Moltmann's permission:

JASON JONES

Dear Mr. Jones,

thank you for your trust. The death of a child is the most
terrible experience parents must make. We lost our first
child at birth and were like paralysed for months, bereft of
all hope.
As answer upon your unanswerable questions, I will tell you
something of my life-story. I grew up in a secular family,
faith and theology was far away from me. I wanted to study
mathmatics and physics, when I was at 16 - 1943 - drafted
to the German army. I survived the bombing of my hometown
Hamburg in July 1943 only by a miracle. My questions were:
Why I am not dead as the friend next to me ? Where is God ?
It took three years until I found the answer. It was in a
poor prisoner-of-war-camp in Scotland. An army chaplain dis-
tributed Bibles. At night I started reading without any
interest. I came to the psalms of lament. Psalm 39 caught my
interest: "I must eat up my suffering in myself. I am a
soujourner as all my forefathers were". Then I read the
gospel of Mark and when I came to the Gethsemani-story and
heard the death cry of Jesus:"My God, why have you forsaken
me ?" I felt the presence of a divine brother who shared
my pain and my forsakenness. I saw my death-and lost -experience
in his great passion-story. I began to pray and to watch
with Jesus in Gethsemani and learned:"Only the suffering
God can help", as Bonhoeffer told us from his Gestapo-cell.
Later I understood that not only Christ is suffering under
the silence of God; the God whom he called "Abba, dear father"
must have suffered too under the bereavement of his only
beloved son."God is the fellow-sufferer who understands"
wrote Alfred North Whitehead (a famous mathematician) in his
book "Process and Reality", when he lost his only son in a
car-eccident in the age of 21.

```
We can find no answer to the Why-question but we can survive
with open wounds when we feel the presence of the suffering
Christ who died withan open question.In his passion we can
```
(God)
```
also see the suffering of God and feel how God is bearing
us. Behind the cross of Christ we see the morning of the
resurrection dawning. The suffering with Christ gives us this
hope.

Dear brother in Christ: I know how poor my answer to your
crying letter is. We are struggling with the dark side of
God like Jacob at the Jabbokriver. When the morning comes we
```
(But)
```
are limping but blessed.

        Friede sei mit Dir und Deiner Familie !


        yours
```

Jürgen Moltmann

"Limping but blessed." That was the perfect way to describe how I felt. Grieving parents cling to hope by looking at other parents who have experienced the same pain and are able to survive and continue to have a good life, so when I read that he was also a bereaved parent, I trusted his words even more, knowing he had wrestled with some of the same questions I had.

All my life, God was stoic and distant, only expressing disappointment with my sin or approval with my good behavior. The most common example of God's love for us was God sacrificing his son on a cross, which didn't leave me feeling warm and fuzzy.

But a God who is close to me and feels betrayal, pain, and sadness is a truer version of God than I had known before. After all, Jesus cried out expressing exactly how I was feeling: "Why have you forsaken me?" There were no words in the Bible I related to more. I felt forsaken. I felt tricked. I felt abandoned by God. Jesus had some of those same feelings, so it must be okay for me to feel the same way.

It was reaffirming that Professor Moltmann referenced another bereaved parent in his letter, One who had lost a son and was suffering with us. If people who have experienced the same pain believe in a God who suffers with them, then there must be some truth there for me.

Professor Moltmann eloquently described a new way of thinking about my suffering and grief: "We can find no answer to the Why question but we can survive with open wounds when we feel the presence of the suffering Christ who died with an open God question."

We can find some hope in the Christ who suffers with us. Those of us who experience terrible tragedies and pain find connection with a God who feels what we feel and enters into our horrific realities.

We are limping but blessed.

7

LIMPING BUT BLESSED

Two years after the accident, I still had open questions, and I was still angry with God and the church. I still had faith, but it was full of bitterness. Jürgen Moltmann and the other pastors and theologians I'd contacted—Tony Jones, Mike Stavlund, Nicholas Wolterstorff, Dan Allender—had helped me wrap my mind around what had happened, but my heart was still hard toward God. They answered my intellectual questions, but my spirit was still disturbed.

When Brea asked me to attend church, I responded with cynicism, trying to get out of it. I couldn't listen to any more preaching or songs that declared God's goodness. But losing my faith would mean significant change in all aspects of my life.

Believing in God and living as a Christian had permeated all of who I was, and was a part of nearly all my relationships. My entire extended family is Christian, my friends are Christian, and my wife and children are Christian. What would it mean if I stopped believing in God?

I knew my family wouldn't abandon me, but they would be concerned. My biggest fear was that they would think less of me because of my loss of faith. And I realized we didn't have any friends that were not Christian. It would be very difficult to stop going to church altogether because it would mean losing a connection with our friends and community. I wanted to keep my friendships, but I wasn't getting anything out of church except frustration.

I wasn't hopeful, either, that a new church would have the answers I was looking for. I would likely disagree with some part of the theology of any church we attended, so we decided not to leave our current church.

I considered simply staying home while Brea and the girls went to church, but this made me feel like a bad dad and husband. Brea was going to church with the girls, and she expected me to go with them. I didn't like the thought of my family going somewhere without me. What would people think of me? What kind of husband stays home? What kind of example am I for my children? I also didn't want to be away from them or distance myself from them. So, I had to figure out how to move forward.

My solution was to fake it. I didn't think I had much to lose by just going through the motions at church. At most, I would lose an hour of my Sunday, but at least I'd be with my family. It was still important to me for our daughters to be grounded in faith. Even in my disbelief, I wanted my children to have the benefits of a life of faith—the type of faith their mother has.

I was surprised to find that losing my belief wasn't scary (although it never felt comfortable). When I contemplated the fact that there may be no God or afterlife, I actually gained a greater appreciation of how precious every second of life is. But what bothered me most about rejecting a belief in God and the afterlife is that I would never see Jacob again. That stopped me in my tracks. Having hope and faith sustains all of us through insurmountable heartache, which is why I so wanted to believe in God. I wanted it to be easy. But it wasn't.

Because I was experiencing what seemed like deafening silence from God, the existence of a sovereign God didn't seem logical or rational, and God wasn't offering me any evidence to believe.

TIRED OF FIGHTING

In April 2014, nearly three years after Jacob's accident, I felt like it was time for me to spend some time alone and deal with my troubled spirit. I had hardly spoken a word to God or prayed at all in those three years. I had been so angry for so long, and I didn't want anything to do with God. Inside there was something pulling me toward this time alone. Similar to the impulse to reach out to an old friend after a long time without speaking, I felt ready to reach out to God again to see if we could move forward. I needed to determine whether I would ever have faith again.

One of my favorite places to relax is along the Frio River in central Texas. My family has been going there for decades, and it's a quiet place in the springtime. I decided to rent a small cabin by myself for the weekend and do some hiking and reading, and also to address my faith. I still had so many questions. Much of my frustration and anger came from me feeling like God had abandoned me, and from feeling that I'd believed a fraud my whole life.

I arrived in the late afternoon on Friday. There were about ten cabins scattered in a pecan grove with a river several hundred yards away. The Frio River lives up to its Spanish name—it's cold. It's clear enough to see your feet even if the water is up to your chest. This section of the river is crowded during the summers, but in April it's quiet and serene. When I checked in, I noticed there were only a handful of other guests staying in cabins, so I knew I was in for a quiet stay.

After I got settled in and unpacked, I figured I would go for a walk and reflect on my experience over the last few years. Paula had told me that the best thing to do was to expect nothing—not to try to force false feelings, or I might find myself disappointed at the end of the weekend because I didn't accomplish something.

None of my beliefs about God seemed to be working, so I started from scratch—trying to put the pieces of my understanding of God back together one question at a time.

I started out on my walk with my first real prayer in a very long time: "God, here I am. Now what? What do we do now? You know I feel like you have hurt me and my family. I'm so sick of you not being here or giving me some peace about all of this."

I really wasn't expecting some manna-from-heaven moment on the banks of the Frio River. But suddenly, I felt a wave of emotion, and I started sobbing. I was at the end of my rope emotionally, and I was exhausted. Walking on a farm road alone in the middle of the day, I cried out to God. I was done fighting, tired of wrestling with God. Like Jacob at the Jabbok River, I had been fighting with God so long and I was ready to give up. I had fought as hard as I could for three years, but to no avail. I still had no answers as to why this had happened to my son.

As I cried, I felt a sense of peace. I was releasing the burden I'd been carrying. I needed to let go of the need to find logical answers to all my questions. I needed to release the analytical side of me that needed a solution to my problem. The surrender did not feel like defeat. Rather, it felt like I had been in a battle and there was nothing left inside me to give. That weekend didn't end up being a mountaintop experience where Jesus spoke to me, and I didn't find answers to all of my questions. But, I did have a feeling that it was okay to lay down this frantic search for why God had allowed Jacob to die.

WHERE IS GOD WHEN IT HURTS?

The word *intervention* assumes the intervening person or object is coming from somewhere else. If God is an interventionist God, then it assumes God is breaking through into our world to take action. I've used this language before in describing God's action, and it's the common way of thinking about miracles: "God must have intervened to save their life."

I have an hour-long commute to work every day, and one of my favorite things to do to pass time is listen to podcasts. One morning, I was listening to Rob Bell's podcast titled "God Part 3." In it, he was discussing the misunderstanding behind the question of why God doesn't do anything, or intervene, when there is so much suffering in the world. He explained that much of our problem with God is that we think God is somewhere else. Our understanding of God depends on *where* we think God is. If God is far away, then we think God has to intervene or come down and do something about it. But, there are also plenty of verses in the Bible that describe God as being with us, near us, and in us.

Bell described it this way: If God is here with us, then there's no intervening to be done. God is already experiencing the same suffering and pain we are. God is with us in the pain—not an absentee God, but rather a co-sufferer. That's a lot like what Moltmann wrote me in his letter.

My whole life I had thought of God as somewhere else. I never realized how much this affected my theology until I heard it put in these words. It made total sense to me. We talk of a God up there. Our prayers are sent up. There are some verses that seem to conflict with the closeness of God, though:

I am coming soon (Revelation 3:11).

For God so loved the world that He sent his only son (John 3:16).

Better is one day in your courts than thousands elsewhere (Psalm 84:10).

I grew up thinking I was going to heaven to be with God, which meant that God wasn't with me here and now. When I prayed, my prayers were directed to God up there, not down here with me. I had always thought that when I prayed for God to do something, it meant that God had to break through or come down and do something. I always imagined some distance between God and myself—a distance caused by sin. This is an incomplete way of looking at God; it focuses too much on trying to get God to do something, to be with us, and to help us. Rather, what if God is right here with us all the time even if we haven't been aware of it?

In Rob Bell's podcast he went on to discuss the story about Jacob in Genesis 28:10–22. In a dream, God tells Jacob how he will take care of him and describes how he will bless his future. When Jacob wakes up, he says, "Surely the Lord is in this place, and I was not aware of it." He talks of a God who was here all along but he didn't realize it.

This means God is in you and me, and we are all connected. If God is in all, then God is in all of creation. God is in the pebbles you walk on, the flowers you pick, the trees giving you shade, and every organism and animal on earth. Grasping the reality of this totally changed the way I think about how God is working in the world. It means God was experiencing the pain and suffering our son Jacob was feeling. God was experiencing the deepest pain and agony Brea and I were feeling in our darkest moments. God wasn't watching from afar, but God was in us, experiencing it with us.

And, if God is in all and through all, then what is the need for God to intervene? This seems like the wrong question to ask of a God who is with us always. And yet, I still wondered why God doesn't stop bad things from happening if he has the power to do so.

DID GOD CAUSE OR ALLOW THIS?

Even though I gained a better understanding of God's presence from Rob Bell and Jürgen Moltmann, I still had unanswered questions. After all, in Moltmann's letter to me he wrote, "We must live with an open God question." I resigned myself to the idea that I may never find good answers to my unanswered questions.

Then, one day while looking on my phone for another podcast to listen to, I ran across an interview of Thomas J. Oord on the Homebrewed Christianity Podcast about his new book, *The Uncontrolling Love of God.*

Oord explained the theological model he called "essential kenosis," which he had outlined in his book:[1]

> *The model of God as essentially kenotic says God's eternal nature is uncontrolling love. Because of love, God necessarily provides freedom/agency to creatures, and God works by empowering and inspiring creation toward well-being. God also necessarily upholds the regularities of the universe because those regularities derive from God's eternal nature of Love. Randomness in the world and creaturely free will are genuine, and God is not a dictator mysteriously pulling the strings. God never controls others. But God sometimes acts mirac-*

---

1. Thomas Jay Oord, *The Uncontrolling Love of God: An Open and Radical Account of Providence* (Downers Grove, IL: IVP Academic, 2015), 94.

ulously, in non-coercive ways. God providentially
guides and calls all creation toward love and beauty.

So if God is first and foremost a God of love, then
God moves out of love first, not power or control.
For many, it's controversial, even heretical to talk
of God's power being limited in any way. At first
glance, this model of God made a lot of sense to me,
but it was not something I felt comfortable talking
openly about with friends and family because I
thought people would just argue with me.

The verse Oord hangs much of his framework on
is 2 Timothy 2:13: "If we are unfaithful, he remains
faithful—for he cannot deny himself." Love does not
control. It doesn't exert its will or power over the
other. If God's nature is essentially love, then God
is not controlling. Oord contends that out of God's
very nature he cannot control because he cannot
deny who he is.

Where love (or God) is present, control of the
other does not and cannot exist. We are creatures
who are loved by God. We are not robots who are
controlled by God's force.

John Wesley, one of the founders of the
Methodist movement, wrote, "Were human liberty
taken away, men would be as incapable of virtue as
stones. Therefore (with reverence be it spoken) the

Almighty himself cannot do this thing. He cannot thus contradict himself, or undo what he has done."[2]

One theological framework that has gained ground over recent years to defend God in the face of suffering and evil is called Open Theism. Its advocates argue that God doesn't intervene to stop evil in this world because the future is open and therefore unknowable, even by God. God is experiencing time just as we are.

The problem with open theism, Oord argues in his book, is that this still leaves open the possibility that God could do something to prevent evil. If God has the power to limit himself initially, then God could still use his power to un-limit himself if he wanted to stop evil and suffering, but chooses not to. Ultimately, this still leaves God on the hook for not stopping evil and suffering.

Using our parent analogy, would God be considered a good parent? If I had the knowledge and power to stop Jacob's accident and didn't, I would have been prosecuted for negligence due to my inaction.

Why is it that we don't hold God accountable for *inaction*? A common prayer is that God forgive us for

2. John Wesley, "On Divine Providence," Sermon LXXII in *The Works of the Reverend John Wesley, A. M.*, Volume II (New York: Waugh & Mason, 1833), 103.

"things done and left undone." But why does God get a free pass for things that he has left undone? That is a question that has continued to haunt me.

THOSE PESKY MIRACLES

When I've discussed God's power or possible self-limitation with others, the conversation invariably turns to the subject of miracles. If God is unable to intervene with his power, then how do you explain events that seem to be miraculous?

Under the essential kenosis model, Oord provides an answer as to why God seems to intervene in this world in some cases, and doesn't intervene in other cases. He explains that the only way God can intervene is with cooperation from creation. There must be a desire or request from creation in order for God to do something. God is not going to act or intervene in a situation, unless there is room for God to work in cooperation with creation to achieve an outcome. The key is, the object of coercion must cooperate with God. God, out of love, can't use his power to control the object.

As I read through Oord's book, I was still confused as to why God didn't cause a miracle to happen when we prayed over Jacob while we were doing CPR. I didn't understand why God didn't wake me up or put it into my mind to lock the doors that day. After all, we were cooperating with God by praying and fervently asking for Jacob to live. There was no time in our life when we or Jacob more urgently needed God. If God is working from a place of essential love and waiting for us to cooperate with him, then this was a legitimate test of that thesis.

After finishing Oord's book, I emailed him the following questions:

1. Why didn't our prayer work as we were doing CPR on Jacob? Brea and I were both praying for Jacob to be healed, which would be considered "cooperating" with God. We were asking God to use his power to bring Jacob back.

2. Why wouldn't God wake me up or give me some thought to lock the doors that day?

In short, his response was that there were other agents, factors, and organisms involved in these situations, and God could not completely control all of them. He explained that Jacob and I are not just simply minds. We have bodies with thousands upon thousands of agents, organisms, and organs that cannot be controlled by God without cooperation.

As for my question about waking me up, he said, "If God could override the human body's need for sleep by controlling it in some way, God should awaken every person who is about to be robbed in the middle of the night. But we know this doesn't happen."

In regard to why my prayer over Jacob while we were doing CPR didn't work he said, "As you worked on Jacob, there were obviously factors in his body that were beyond the capacity for the kind of cooperation necessary for this resuscitation."

Tom's responses made sense, and his theory explained why miracles are still possible in light of a God whose ability to exert power is limited. The essential kenosis model helped me articulate the answer I was looking for as to how Jacob could die in an accident if there was a good, loving, powerful God.

Jacob and I both have our own unique wills that God will not and cannot control, born out of his love for us. Jacob decided to go outside and get in the car. God cannot force his will on inanimate objects like the car door, or on Jacob to keep him from getting in the car. I was tired and my body is made up of additional organs and organisms that wanted rest as well. God couldn't force his will on my mind or body to "intervene." Therefore, God wasn't going to stop either one of us.

Finally, my prayer to save Jacob didn't "work" because Jacob had been in the car for too long to have been able to survive or be resuscitated. His body had been too damaged to respond, and God was unable to force his body to come back from such damage.

WHAT MY FAITH LOOKS LIKE NOW

Doubting is now part of my faith.

To be frank, I wish believing in God were easier. I don't like being a doubter, and in many ways I feel like blind faith is an easier way to live life. But now I think doubting is part of my faith and there is no authentic faith that doesn't include questions.

I believe everyone doubts, but not everyone feels comfortable admitting it out loud. Doubt seems to be an integral part of the human experience—and it's a vital part of spirituality—so I think we shouldn't be silent and alone in our doubts. We need to create safe spaces in every Christian church and community for people to share their frustrations, doubts, and questions about their faith.

My faith is still unsettled and uncertain. Even though most days I feel totally mystified by all of it, I still want to rebuild my faith. I want to feel like I've found God again. Until then, I keep searching and hoping that I land on some truths I can trust again.

Right now, this is what I believe or at least want to believe:

I believe in a God who is with us.

Instead of thinking God is somewhere else, I now hold on to the God who is "above all, through all, and in all" (Ephesians 4:13). God is a good God who is here with me and in me and all around me, in and through all things I encounter.

I don't have to feel like God is distant or unreachable. I don't need to try to get God to pay attention to me by my actions or words. I can rest in the fact that God is right here with me while I write this sentence on my computer in a coffee shop. God is experiencing this with me and co-creating this book with me in his uncontrolling love.

Believing in a God who is in and through all of us also gives me empathy for all things in creation—especially other people. I admit, I'm still not very good at this.

We're all suffering or wounded but we are also the extension of God to one another. My extended hand reaching down to help someone else is God working through me to provide help. This is God working in us, with our cooperation. It's exciting to take on this divine responsibility to help others. It's not all God making things happen, but it takes our cooperation as well. It makes it even more important to act for the benefit of creation.

I believe in a God who suffers with us.

There is something much more comforting about a God who is suffering with us than one who is watching from afar. Moltmann writes, "When God becomes man in Jesus of Nazareth, he not only enters into the finitude of man, but in his death on the cross also enters into the situation of man's god forsakenness. . . . He humbles himself and takes upon himself the eternal death of the godless and the godforsaken, so that all the godless and the godforsaken can experience communion with him."[3]

I pray again because I think we are co-creating this life with God by his non-coercive love.

After Jacob's accident, I prayed every day and night for God to give us strength, to give us peace, and to give me answers as to why he would allow this to happen. I don't know how much my prayers helped because the pain was so deep. The longer I went on without answers, the angrier I got.

I gave up and stopped praying. I didn't pray for three years. I didn't see any point to it. Part of me didn't even believe there was a God. And the sliver of me that was still holding on to faith believed in

3. Jürgen Moltmann, *The Crucified God: 40th Anniversary Edition* (Minneapolis: Fortress Press, 2015), 414.

a God who was watching from afar and not able to help.

Eventually, I did come to the conclusion that God loves me and didn't cause Jacob's accident, but it took a very long time to get to that point.

But if God can't exert power, then what is the use in praying? I thought God was somehow limited or self-limited and was unable to intervene at all, so prayer seemed unnecessary. At least it became unnecessary in the way I'd thought about it before. But with my new understanding of God, there's still a reason to pray. I now pray to connect with God through centering prayer or just quietly sitting focusing on God.

I find myself praying less often than I used to, but my prayers are more meaningful, at least to me. My prayers are less about what I want and more about being quiet. If something comes to my mind or I would like a certain outcome, then I'll ask for it with hope that it makes a difference. If one of my family members is sick, then I will pray for them to be healed. If I am anxious about a situation, I will ask God for help. I don't pray with an expected outcome, though. I simply pray with hope that through God's non-coercive love, things will improve.

I still struggle with God, but now I struggle with hope.

8

DON'T LEAVE
THE FUNERAL
EARLY

As the week led up to Jacob's funeral service, I felt like an alien in my own body. The event so changed me that it felt as though I was someone else. I also felt an increasingly profound sense of loneliness. Even though millions of parents have experienced the same pain and grief as I have, I felt as if no one else on the planet, except for Brea, could relate to me. It felt like I was on an island, wondering if I would ever be comfortable around people again.

Although we couldn't imagine it at the time, once the shock wore off months down the road, things actually got much worse emotionally. But, in those initial weeks and months the shock shielded us and allowed us to function and communicate with all the people that were visiting us.

I was so thankful for how many people came to see us that first week.

At Jacob's life celebration on Thursday, June 16, 2011, we arrived at the church about an hour early to sit and collect ourselves. Some friends we hadn't seen in years came back to the room where we were waiting to tell us how sorry they were.

Our family decided to wear casual clothes to the life celebration because we wanted to dress in what we thought Jacob would like the most. He wouldn't have wanted to dress up and be in a suit and tie. So, Brea wore a favorite sun dress of Jacob's and I wore a pair of khaki pants and a polo-style shirt. It was casual, which I imagine shocked some people. But it felt right for us, and looking back, I'm glad we did it.

I'll never forget the scene when we walked into the sanctuary that day. Brea and I held hands, each of us holding hands with one of the girls. Brea had been holding on to the little blue bear Jacob slept with his entire life. Jacob's little bear was definitely his security blanket. When he got into bed at night he would have two things with him: his pacifier and his little bear. The bear was pretty worn and ragged. Jacob would rub his nose against one corner of the bear to comfort himself while he was lying down.

Brea had a hold of that bear through the entire service, and for the next year the bear was in bed with us. The little bear that had comforted him during his life was now comforting us.

I was taken aback at how many people showed up to Jacob's funeral. Many of the people in attendance had never met Jacob, but they were friends and acquaintances, there to support us. The church was full, and people were lined up along the walls.

After the service, we were swarmed with people extending their condolences. Most of them just wanted to give us a hug and to tell us they loved us. So many people were lined up to talk with us that the pastor had to pull me away when it was time to go to the graveside service.

This was a tragedy. This was our suffering. And people showed up in droves. People came to be with us and they supported us so well on that day. I'll never forget some of the hugs, the words spoken, the hands on my shoulder, the tears shed, the hundreds of "I'm sorries" I heard. From the very beginning we knew we had an amazing network of friends and family that we will never be able to repay.

I know now how important it is in those initial days and weeks after a loss to reach out to others. Even though we felt isolated and alone inside, when people showed up we felt loved and cared for despite our isolation. We knew people were going to walk with us through this pain. Thank God for that and thank God people showed up.

JACOB'S TREE

On the Tuesday after Jacob died, I saw a truck driving up the driveway with the logo of the company I work for. Two of the founders of the company and one of my co-workers came to visit. As they walked up to me, I started crying, and so did they. I hugged them. "I'm so sorry," they said. "Whatever you need, let us know." I appreciated what they said, but I was most thankful for their presence.

When people came to visit us, I can't remember much of what they said or how they said it. But I can tell you, I vividly remember their comforting presence in our home.

One of the most important lessons I learned going through this was how important it was for people to be with us. No one says exactly the right thing when someone is hurting. That's perfectly okay. The most important thing you can do is to bear witness to their pain.

And that has led me to something I believe with everything inside me: we don't heal alone.

I wrote earlier about our flashbacks and how difficult Sundays had become for us. When we talked to Paula about this, she asked us if there was something we do to distract ourselves on Sunday evenings. She suggested that we invite friends or family to come spend time with us so we weren't stuck inside our own heads. Brea and I talked about it and decided to start having a standing dinner with friends and family every Sunday evening.

We put the word out: "If you are available, please come have dinner with us." We couldn't have been more blessed by the willingness of people to come be with us. Some Sundays we had a house full and some we had one person. We had a community of people who stood by us when we needed them most. With each passing week, the people who spent time with us brought a little more light into our life when it was filled with darkness. The more people we had around us, the more opportunity for laughter and joy, which brought us hope that we would find a way to the other side of this.

On one of those Sundays, some of our closest friends drove up with a little tree in the back of their truck. They told us it was a tree for Jacob and that we could all plant it together. After "Jacob's Tree" was planted we stood around while one of our friends read a dedication she'd written. This gesture and act of kindness touched us deeply. It's something that we will never forget. Every time I look at that tree, I do think of Jacob. But, I also remember that we're not alone and that we have people who care for us and love us.

In the busyness of our lives we often neglect building friendships. The older we get, the more that work and the demands of raising children take up the bulk of our time and focus. And, when life happens, we wonder why no one is around to help. At our core, all of us are afraid of being alone. And, some of our loneliest times can be during our darkest moments.

As humans, we all yearn to feel loved and cared for. The people who surrounded us day after day, for months, are one of the biggest reasons we were able to heal the way we did. Without them, there is no way we would be where we are today. We are truly blessed to have such loving and faithful people around us.

Not only is it wonderful to enjoy friendships and family during good times, but those relationships become even more important to help hold us up in the bad times. This is a two-way street. Your family and friends are going to need you too. And, the absolute best thing you can give them is your simple presence. Sit with them and hold them when they need it. They won't remember what you said. But, they'll never forget that you showed up.

DON'T LEAVE US BEHIND

But the funeral ended. People went home, and they went on with their lives. The Sunday dinners became sporadic. The visitors stopped visiting. The pastors went on to help other people in crisis. And other than close family, no one seemed to miss Jacob anymore—at least not like we did.

Unfortunately, Brea and I did experience a distancing of some of our relationships as the first year passed. We noticed that everyone else returned to normal life, yet our new life didn't feel very normal at all. Every moment for us was a moment without Jacob.

Taking the kids to their first day of school and seeing other siblings walking with their parents was gut-wrenching. I hated walking into church and seeing families taking their toddlers into Sunday school. The worst—and this still feels weird every time—is going to a restaurant and telling them we need a table for four instead of five.

The world just kept moving forward, but we were stuck in grief. The pain of losing a child never goes away and the grief lasts much longer than people expect. It takes years to get your bearings back.

When people stopped coming around or checking in on us, we didn't understand. We thought we may have done or said something wrong. We wondered if we had become too hard to be around for some people. Looking back, I think they couldn't handle being around us anymore. Our pain and sadness were too difficult to witness, and frankly, I can understand getting burned out by it. In the moment, though, it was very painful to have friends stop calling or spending time with us.

The fact is, others do have to move on in life. When I mentioned this feeling in a group therapy session with other grieving parents, many echoed my feelings—this seems to be a universal experience. A number of factors contribute to this. First, we aren't taught very well how to handle grief and death. We're taught to avoid pain and suffering and to pursue happiness. Because of this, we lack skills for helping people who are suffering.

Additionally, I think the pain is too much for some people. They're not wired to provide empathy to others. Others, who are always positive and live in a glass-half-full world, have a difficult time entering into another's grief for too long. Eventually, they want to pull the other person out of their pain for their own sake or they leave because they can't relate to the pain the other is feeling.

Lastly, out of frustration sometimes we leave people who don't seem like they want to get better. You may have experienced this person in your life. A person who has been depressed by something and just refuses to get help after a period of time. They end up getting comfortable with their pain. At some point, we have to heal. Unfortunately, if we don't get help the pain always comes home to roost. It is frustrating as a friend or family member to watch someone who won't get help, so we throw up our hands and walk away.

WHAT I WISH OTHERS KNEW

This isn't an advice book. But allow me to give a little advice anyway. Here's what I learned, and what I will do in the future when I have family or friends who are grieving.

Don't ask, "How can I help?" Just do it.

I don't know how we would have done it without our immediate family members. They moved in with us for two months to care for us and to help with the girls. They cooked our meals. They cleaned our house. They paid our bills. They were our chauffeurs to meetings, school, work, and our first therapy sessions. The best part about their help was they didn't ask what they could do. They just did it. Our brains were so drained that we didn't even have the capacity to think about what could be done or what needed to be done.

I went back to work after three weeks, and the only way I made it there was because my dad drove me. Then he stayed there for hours and drove me back home. He was there. Not just to drive me but for so much more.

We gave our family our checkbook and bills, and they took care of our finances. They did whatever they could to give us rest and to keep us from having to do anything that took brain power because we had nothing to give.

Our family changed entire holiday traditions just for us. The first Christmas without Jacob, we all rented a huge home and everyone traveled from all over Texas to be together. It was a huge sacrifice and a big change for everyone, but it was worth it because we were all able to be together during a very difficult holiday season.

After being around enough other parents who have experienced this pain, I know our family is the exception rather than the rule. We are truly blessed to have a family full of giving and loving people who are generous with their time.

Be consistent about checking in on them for the entire first year.

Our church had a prayer team that sent us letters every couple of weeks saying they were praying for us. Again, it didn't matter what their letter said, it was the fact that they sent a letter at all. Others hadn't forgotten about the pain we were in. Their acknowledgment actually fueled us and gave us hope that we could find healing.

Brea is a stay-at-home mom and when school started that September, Jacob should have still been at home with her. She was not ready to be at home by herself and it was a very difficult, lonely situation for her. Thankfully, one of her friends took time to run with her every morning. It was a simple thing, but it made a gigantic difference.

It really is the little things that people never forget when they are dealing with life's difficulties. You don't have to move mountains; just pick up a pebble.

Talk about and remember their loved one.

Often people are scared or nervous to bring up Jacob to us for fear of upsetting us, making us cry, or making it awkward. I totally get that, and I am appreciative of them considering how it may make us feel. But here's the thing: we are already thinking about him—nearly all the time—especially the first few years after his passing. That first year, I thought about him every single second. I wanted to talk about him and I wanted other people to talk about him.

One of our biggest fears is that people will forget Jacob. I want people to know I have a son. It helps to hear others say his name and bring him up. Yes, we might cry, but that is nothing new if you know us very well.

Ironically, one of the things I'm most self-conscious about recently is the lack of emotion I have when talking about Jacob. I think as a protective mechanism, my mind kind of shuts down so I don't fall apart while talking about him. I often worry whether people think I'm cold or heartless because of the lack of emotion I have when talking about him. Rest assured, I'm a complete basket case and mess just under the surface. Over time, I've just learned how to keep it at bay until I'm by myself where I can let it out.

We want to talk about Jacob, even though it may be painful. And, we are grateful when people are willing to step into that uncomfortable and awkward conversation. The best way to start is: "I remember when Jacob. . . ."

Another tip: send cards and texts on birthdays of the loved one and anniversaries of the death. Those are really hard days and it makes a huge difference to hear from people and to know they are being thought of. Again, it takes very little effort to make someone feel loved and cared for.

We're making it now, five years later, because a lot of family and friends stood by us. Some didn't, maybe because it was too hard or awkward. I understand, but I wish they would have stuck around.

But a lot of others did hang with us. And we had a lot more support than a lot of grieving families have.

When the funeral ends, the grieving just begins. Remember that when someone close to you loses a loved one. And if you're the one in grief, hang on to others for dear life.

9

REDEEMING OUR SUFFERING

I once saw a quote by the ancient Greek philosopher Epictetus: "It's not what happens to you, but how you react to it that matters."

Even when I had a thousand hands holding mine, trying to help me up off the ground, it felt like I was going to be swallowed up by the circumstances I found myself in. But even after I realized that I had something to live for, I wasn't sure I was going to be able to find meaning to push through the depression I was in. I felt heartbroken, betrayed by God, lonely even when surrounded by friends and family, and stuck in a loop I didn't know how to break. You may have felt this way after a loss of your own, a divorce, or a trauma. It's strange that we feel so lonely even though we know there are millions of other people who have experienced the same type of suffering we have. I think we feel this way because the suffering separates us from who we used to be. If it's drastic enough, then the pain changes us, literally. We can't recognize who we are or relate to others the way we used to. We inherently sense that people don't know who we are anymore. We are in many ways a different person.

I gravitated toward grieving parents who had made it through, hoping they would be able to save me from my pain, that they had some secret to living again, and that they must not feel the pain anymore. But after listening to anyone who had suffered deeply, I realized they were not over their pain, they had just figured out how to live with it.

At some point, I realized that I, too, wanted to move on. I wanted to live. This didn't come in an *aha!* moment. I just knew in my heart that I had to for Brea and my girls.

One evening in our grieving parent group, around year two, I said out loud, "I guess I'm going to have to start figuring out what life is going to look like going forward because I guess I'm going to survive this." I feared becoming a victim of my pain. We had witnessed a number of adults who were stuck in childhood trauma or other grieving parents we had met, and I knew I didn't want to live that way.

Grieving and sitting with your suffering for a time is important, but at some point you have to live life.

But, what is it that actually gets you up off the couch or out of bed to face life again? Where does the motivation come from? Like much of my story, I found the answers from the words of someone who had suffered and had shared their life experiences to help push others in the right direction.

REDEMPTION: THE BEST QUESTION

Soon after the accident, Brea and I would start our mornings by sitting on our front porch with friends and family drinking coffee. Then we would go sit and write in our journals. Most of my journaling was me writing out prayers that started to be filled with questions as time went on. As I wrote about in previous chapters, the most common questions started with *Why?*

I was stuck in my own head, asking questions and trying to find an answer that would make sense. I felt like I was stuck on a hamster wheel running after hundreds of answers to questions with no end in sight.

One day I outlined a number of my questions in my journal and I wanted to talk through them with one of our pastors at church, Bill. He had been coming over to visit us daily and I wanted to talk through how God's sovereignty and the presence of so much innocent suffering made no sense to me. I wondered why people were okay with responding to my questions with "You just have to trust God."

Along with a couple of friends, Bill and I sat on our back porch together on a 100-degree Texas evening. We sat outside pretending that it wasn't uncomfortable with plastic cups full of lukewarm wine. I got my journal out and started running through my questions with Bill. My thought was that if anyone was going to give me the answers I had about God, it was going to be an experienced pastor. Bill had also worked as a hospice chaplain for much of his life, so he was not new to grief or listening to a grieving person talk about their disappointments with God. Plus, he had experienced the loss of a child. His infant son died of SIDS over thirty years ago. He also let me ask questions and doubt God out loud without making me feel judged. Theologically, we had many of the same questions about God's sovereignty.

That afternoon, as I started going through my list with Bill, he sat back and listened. He didn't try to rebut my questions. He nodded in recognition of my anger and disillusionment over what had happened. After some time, I finally stopped talking and I waited in fervent anticipation to receive the answers I'd been hoping to find. He sat up a little in his chair and said to me, "Jason, these are all legitimate questions. These are hard questions, and you have every right to ask them. But, *Why?* is not the right question. The only good question you can ask yourself is this: *Now that this has happened, what are you going to do about it?*"

I sat back in my chair and took it in. And I didn't like it. Instead of providing an answer, Bill told me that I was asking the wrong question. I felt a sense of responsibility to Jacob to figure out why this happened. If I don't find out why, then I'm letting Jacob down and letting God off the hook. But I continued to come up empty-handed. There was no good answer. Ultimately, I realized Bill had given me the best question I could ask myself at this point.

What am I going to do now? requires action. This is so important because sometimes our circumstances can paralyze us, and our inaction can leave us wallowing in our sadness or despair, which can lead to depression. By getting our minds and bodies in motion we at least begin to look outside of ourselves and take the focus off of our current state of pain and suffering.

Also, by choosing to use suffering and energy

to do something good, we can redeem some of the circumstance we are in.

Bill had one last thing to say to me about my *Why?* questions that day. He said, "Jason, is there any answer to your questions that would take away any of your pain or sadness?" Without hesitation, I said, "Absolutely not." There does not exist an answer that would make me feel better. Even if I knew why, it wouldn't be a good enough answer to keep me from missing Jacob with every fiber of my being.

So I realized that the start of finding peace and healing again was to ask, *What am I going to do about it?* This question is where we begin to start to redeem the suffering in our lives. The key for me was to stop looking at my own circumstances and my own pain and focus on looking outside of myself. That's when a real shift in a healthy direction happened.

REDEMPTION: FINDING MEANING

In his 1946 bestselling book, *Man's Search for Meaning*, Viktor Frankl writes, "Humans' primary motivation in life is to find a meaning in life. Ultimately, life is not about pursuing happiness or power. But, rather happiness is a byproduct human beings find by living a meaningful life."[1]

A Jewish psychotherapist in Vienna, Viktor Frankl was arrested in 1942 and sent to a concentration camp along with his family members. After surviving the Holocaust he wrote *Man's Search for Meaning*. Frankl had been issued a visa to visit America, knowing the Nazis were already rounding up Jews, starting with the elderly. He was newly married and ready to leave Vienna but didn't want to leave his parents behind. He decided to visit a cathedral to think about what he should do and he asked God for a sign.

Upon his return from the cathedral, his father gave him a piece of rubble that had fallen from one of the synagogues bombed by the Nazis. The rubble turned out to be part of the Ten Commandments, the one about honoring your mother and father. Feeling like that was a clear sign from God, he decided to stay behind and help his mother and father. Tragically, Frankl, his pregnant wife, and his parents were eventually all transported to concentration camps, and only he survived.

American culture is obsessed with finding happiness and reducing any amount of discomfort or pain. But, Frankl's work tells us that we're focused on looking for the wrong thing. His psycho-

1. Viktor Frankl, *Man's Search for Meaning* (Boston: Beacon, 1992), 104.

therapeutic method, Logotherapy, is founded on the belief that our most motivating force is to find a meaning to life. Furthermore, Frankl goes on to say, "It is the very pursuit of happiness, that thwarts happiness."

How do we find more meaning in life? In his book, Frankl gives us three ways it can be found:

1. By having a work to do.

2. By loving someone or something.

3. By redeeming the pain and suffering in life.

Frankl recounts how he put his theory to use by talking with suicidal camp prisoners. Those prisoners who found a purpose to stay alive in the midst of unbearable conditions were much more likely to survive the camp than those who focused on their suffering.

I didn't think I would feel happiness again, and I doubted the possibility of living a good life anymore. But ultimately, finding meaning in helping others is what pulled us forward into healing. Early on, Brea and I became acutely aware of all the pain and suffering in the world, and we had something deep within us calling us to do something. We had found meaning in getting out of bed every day for our daughters. But we needed to find a meaning to live a full life again.

In early 2014, I read something on Donald

Miller's blog about creating a life plan. One of the exercises for this life plan was to name all the negative events in your life and find some positive attribute to that negative event. According to Logotherapy, once you find some positive turn to your trauma, loss, or hurt, it then ceases to be suffering, or at least lessens the suffering a bit.

As I went through this exercise, I had no trouble defining the most difficult time in my life. What I found difficult, and almost insulting, was to find some positive meaning to Jacob's death.

At first, I felt deflated, because I thought maybe this was the one life event that no one could possibly find something positive from. Not only did it feel impossible to come up with something, but it felt wrong—like I was betraying Jacob. But, then I heard Dr. Frankl in an interview say something that gave me a breakthrough. He said, even in the worst of circumstances, like the death of a child, you can still find meaning in the suffering. You can let the suffering teach you.

Something clicked. This pain has taught me something and continues to teach me. Not only does my sharing help others, but I need to share my experiences in order to heal myself. The more I've shared my story and pain with others, the more I share this burden I have inside, instead of carrying it all by myself.

The more we all share our pain with each other, the more healing we can all do in carrying each other's burdens. That's where the deepest and truest human connection happens.

In these most authentic, raw, vulnerable experiences where we are sharing our suffering and difficulties with each other is where I feel God is working and moving inside of us. In these moments, I feel God again.

REDEMPTION: SUPERHERO BALL

After Jacob died, we asked people who wanted to give to a cause in honor of Jacob to give it to Children's Hopechest, a nonprofit that helps orphans in Africa. There was something inside us that was so touched by knowing Jacob's life would continue to make a difference. Partly, we felt like it was our obligation as his parents to make sure our son still mattered to others and that he continued to make a difference. And there was a part of me that was terrified that his life would be forgotten.

These orphans had also experienced pain in their lives, so we felt connected to them through loss and suffering. Because of the way it was affecting our life, one day Brea and I were brainstorming about how we could raise even more support for these orphans and get more involved. Since Jacob was such a big superhero fan, we were trying to figure out how to put Jacob's mark on an event and raise money for Hopechest simultaneously. We decided it should be a family event where adults and children came dressed as their favorite superheroes, and we would have activities for kids, dancing, dinner, and live and silent auctions to raise money. We named the event the Superhero Ball.

In September 2011, we sat down with a handful of friends who wanted to help us put the fundraiser together and we set a date for February 2012. I talked to Hopechest and told them about the idea we had and they were in full support of it. They asked us to think about which area of Africa we wanted to work in.

With the help of hundreds of volunteers, we had four Superhero Balls and raised over $150,000. With that money we were able to fund a number of sustainable projects and personal development initiatives for the community and orphans in Rubanda, Uganda. We set up a microfinance fund, initially for the purpose of helping widows and caretakers of the children in our program to start their own business. Many of them purchased potato seeds and grew potatoes to sell at the markets. The fund was so successful that it has been opened to the entire community and works like a credit union.

We also funded the construction of new restrooms for the Murole Preparatory School in Rubanda. When we first visited Murole, we noticed all the kids running to a hill where they would disappear. Standing downwind of the hill, we quickly realized where the kids were going: their outdoor latrine. It was not a big deal to them, but improving those "restrooms" is something we wanted to do for them. Additionally, many of the children needed new clothes and shoes, so we bought them all new shoes and uniforms.

We wanted to fund projects that would be sustainable, so we tried to come up with ideas that would continue to generate income after the initial investment. We decided to help them start a piggery. We bought several pigs they could breed and then sell the piglets.

One of the projects I'm most proud of is called Jacob's House. When we asked the leadership in Uganda to prioritize projects to be funded, they said that the kids needed a place to stay overnight because many of them had to walk too far from their homes to school every day.

In Uganda, there's still witchcraft practiced, and

witch doctors sometimes abduct little boys and cut off their genitals in an attempt to heal adults who have HIV. Most of those abductions take place in the early morning or at night when children are walking alone. Many of the children were having to walk long distances to attend school, so this jumped to the top of the list of projects to fund. If we could help prevent these horrific abductions and give the kids a safe place to sleep near the school, it was a no-brainer. We officially opened Jacob's House in June 2014, and it now houses over a hundred orphaned boys.

Each year we held the Superhero Ball, we had more and more people attend. At the last Superhero Ball over six hundred attended and we raised a record amount. The night was always about finding a way to come together as a community of people to help these children on the other side of the world. We knew we were loved, by the outpouring of people who wanted to help. Some people helped because they loved Jacob and he had touched their life. Others helped because they knew our family and wanted to support us. And there were total strangers who just wanted to bring their family to an event where they knew they were a part of something big happening in our little town.

It didn't matter that we were all there for

different reasons. The one unifying reason we were there was our desire to be a part of something bigger than ourselves. We are all searching to find meaning, which is ultimately found outside of ourselves.

Redemption: Visiting Uganda

Shortly after the first fundraiser, something started tugging at me to go visit the children we were supporting in Uganda. So once we had raised enough money to do some really important projects and we got a number of children sponsored, we then decided to take our first trip to Uganda in October 2012.

I'd hardly traveled outside of Texas, much less been on the other side of the world. One of the things that affected me most on the first trip to Uganda was the extent of poverty and how hard these kids' lives were, yet they seemed content and genuinely happy. Being in that environment depressed me at first. It was overwhelming. I think that our overstimulated spoiled lifestyle sends us into shock when we find ourselves in a simpler, more relaxed environment. That first trip was more about being introduced to the community and connecting as best we could in a week. We crammed as many activities as we could into five days. It solidified our commitment to helping these children and putting personal relationships to the cause we had set in motion to honor Jacob's life.

We made a second trip in June 2014. Jacob's House had been completed, and we were going to be there for the commemoration and grand opening of the dormitory named after Jacob. Knowing it was going to be a difficult trip, I wanted to make sure I had close friends and family there with me to help me get through it. Part of me was actually dreading the trip. To me, this commemoration and ceremony had a stamp of finality on it. There would be no denying Jacob wasn't here when we hung his picture up on this dorm and named it after him. I was incredibly proud of Jacob and honored to be naming something after him. But the last thing I ever wanted to do in my life was be in another country naming a building after my son who had died. Honestly, I was incredibly sad to be there opening this dormitory, and I'm hesitant to admit, a little resentful too.

As we prepared to go on our trip, one of the items I wanted to make sure we had perfect was the picture of Jacob we were going to put up on the outside wall of the dormitory. All the children in the community would see his face every day hanging on that wall, so I wanted to make sure we put one up that Brea and I liked. It had to be transportable in our luggage without getting damaged, and we made contingency plans to make sure that if any piece of luggage was going to successfully make it to Uganda it was going to be the suitcase with Jacob's picture in it. I didn't care if any of my clothes or the other items made it to Uganda, as long as that picture made it. It may sound weird, but I felt like I was protecting that picture almost like it was him.

The day of the opening of Jacob's House came, and I was full of mixed emotions. We had to bring all the tools with us to secure his picture up on the concrete wall because there are no tools in the village. No good hammers, screws, nails, or wall fasteners. Nothing. So, we had to bring all of it with us. As we drove up, there was more activity around the school than usual. Decorations were being put up and a big tent and chairs were out in the middle of the soccer field where the ceremony would be held. The magnitude of the event was starting to hit home. For a brief moment, I let down my guard and thought, "This is all for Jacob." My emotions started coming to the surface, but I refused to let myself cry.

Our first task at hand was getting his picture up on the dormitory wall.

I found the suitcase we had used to transport Jacob's picture. I went over and unzipped it. When I looked at his beautiful face I fought back more tears.

That picture felt like a piece of him that I had brought to Uganda and was going to leave there. Many of the people in the village had heard Jacob's name before, but they had not seen him.

My brother noticed I was having trouble, so he told me to take a break and walk around for a minute if I needed to. The guys all worked together to get the picture up, centered it, and secured it to the wall. It looked wonderful. Then they added letters to spell "Jacob's House" above his picture. I was so grateful to these men who pitched in to get his picture up. It meant so much to me and I would have never been able to do it without them.

The ceremony started, and I was still torn. Part of me was celebrating Jacob's House, but another part of me felt like I was at another funeral for him. After several local leaders and politicians spoke, it was time to do a formal ribbon cutting. As we walked over to the dormitory, I could feel the weight of the moment, and I knew we were getting close to ending what was a long journey to get Jacob's House funded, constructed, and now opened. One of the local ministers from Uganda who was part of the ceremony walked up to me and put his arm around me. I couldn't hold back my emotion anymore. God bless him for putting his arm around me, and when I started crying and he said, "Stay strong, you can do this." He was very sweet. But, I had been staying as strong as I could for the last few days leading up to this moment and it all started pouring out right then.

Norman, the founder of the Murole Preparatory School, gave us scissors to cut the ribbon, and I had a minister on one side of me and a politician on the other. I could barely see the ribbon through the tears. The three of us walked up to the ribbon, each of the men put their hands on mine, and we cut the ribbon together. It was such a surreal moment. Then I glanced at Jacob's picture on the wall. "Yes, my little man. You're the reason I'm here. I'm so proud of you and I'm so thankful for you." I felt pride well up inside me, overtaking the sadness I had been carrying. I was so thankful to be helping these people and these orphans because I have a son I love so deeply.

Our love for Jacob is not gone because now it flows through so many more people. I often imagine the smiles of the children who walk past Jacob's picture every day, thankful for this little boy with red hair who inspired hundreds of people to help them with their education, food, and a safe place to sleep every night.

REDEMPTION: FINDING HAPPINESS

On this same trip I met a very special young man. His name is Innocent. After one of our impromptu photo sessions, Innocent stood with me and watched me scroll through the pictures on my phone. I showed him pictures of our house, which was actually a little embarrassing. At best, most families live in dirt-floor structures, with no electricity or running water in the village we were visiting. So, here I am showing him a picture of my house with a swimming pool in the back yard. He seemed quite perplexed as to why I had a giant pool of water in my back yard.

As I was showing him pictures of Brea, Kendall, and Kelsey, school events, and holidays, he says, "Wait. Who is that?" With hesitation and a knot in my throat, I said, "That's Jacob." He looks at me with one of the most serious faces I've ever seen.

"That's Jacob?" he asked.

"Yes," I replied.

I could sense the reverence emanating from his deep brown eyes. It was like time slowed down and we didn't say anything to each other. We were in the middle of a field with hundreds of other kids running around, and I can't remember hearing anything else. We locked eyes. His eyes started welling up with tears and in that moment we connected on another level.

In that moment all language, nationality, and age barriers were broken. It was something I'll never forget.

In his eyes and demeanor, I could sense compassion and empathy. He knows what loss is like, and I could tell that he hurt for me. There was an indescribable and unspoken connection of love that somehow came from a fifteen-year-old boy who had never met Jacob and had only known me for a very short time. With stoic grace he whispered to me with a slight accent, "Oh Jacob, I love him. He is a good boy." I nearly crumbled. Then he took his finger and touched the screen to rub Jacob's hair. "Look at his hair. It's orange!" he said.

"Yep, you're right," I said. "It's orange." And we laughed together.

Innocent had heard the story of Jacob and knew the new dormitory he was now sleeping in was named after him. Jacob's life is giving this fifteen-year-old boy shelter on the other side of the world.

Encounters like this one continue to give me purpose and meaning. In these moments is where I find a sliver of redemption of our pain and grief. No amount of good in the world can make up for Jacob's absence or take away the sadness we feel, but it makes life a little more bearable one day at a time. As these small moments turned into days, we slowly began to find more meaning in life by helping others.

Then even in the midst of our pain, something we didn't know we would ever feel again showed up: Joy.

EPILOGUE: THIS ISN'T THE END

When we first started talking to other bereaved parents about their experiences, many of them told us that the second year is the hardest. I think we experience more profound pain during the second year because the shock eventually wears off and we wake up and realize that we're going to have to live with this the rest of our life.

Brea and I both agree, however, that the first year for us was the worst. Since Jacob was only three and we had been caring for him and spending time with him all day, every day, his absence was so obvious, profound, and life-altering. We felt lost without him at our side every moment of the day. The first year is full of denying the reality and finality of the death. For months I prayed for God to bring Jacob back, as if that was somehow possible. The days of that first year were agonizingly long; it was an immense battle, both physically and emotionally, to get through the sixteen hours of being awake. Going to sleep at night was the only respite from the pain.

Years two through four are what I call the lost years. Our minds were consumed with thinking about Jacob and our concern for healing our family. For me, much of my activity in the day was to distract myself. Whether it was work, trying to figure out how to fundraise, or write, I put my mind to task to keep it focused on something other than my grief. Some of the distraction was good and useful. Unfortunately, other parts of my life suffered—most notably, my daughters. They didn't get enough of me for several formative years. My lack of time in parenting them was collateral damage from Jacob's death.

I don't know if I could have done anything different because much of the time away from them was spent in therapy. I'd love to have been able to put time on pause so I could spend the time I wanted to with them. But, life does not stop or slow down. It marches on, with no regard to our circumstances.

Now that five years have passed, I feel like we have found our bearings as a family. When I think about the moment Brea and I were lying on the floor in our bedroom together, I realize how far we've come. We are now dreaming about our future again. We want to experience a full, long life instead of hoping we will die soon. We want to see our daughters married; we want the experience of holding and caring for grandkids.

But, I don't ever want to get over Jacob's death—it's not something I want to leave behind me or forget in order to make life more manageable. The despair and depression has eased, though there are still times it brings me to my knees. Being a bereaved parent is a lifelong sentence of learning how to deal with the emotional ups and downs that come with the death of a child.

LESSONS FROM JACOB

I talk differently about God now. Over the last five years I've toned down my religious jargon. Not because I think I'm right in the way I think about God, but exactly the opposite. Now more than ever, I'm less sure of how God works. It is a mystery in many ways, but I feel comfortable with that now more than ever. I think I used to fool myself into thinking I had everything figured out. Or, that I had to have everything figured out. Now, I freely admit when I don't understand. And, most of my answers about God start with, "I think or I believe." I don't "know" much of anything for sure.

Honestly, I'm still a little frustrated and hurt by

God. I'm working through it. I think in some ways, I still blame God. So, it is harder to "want" to pursue God. I don't think God caused this, so I'm heading in the right direction to figure out how to relate to God, but it's not what it used to be, and I'm okay with that.

There are a number of lessons Jacob's life and death have taught me.

Our legacy will be measured by the love we share and by the investment we put in others. No one is going to remember how many toys I accumulated, the hours I put in at work, or the title that came after my name. So much of our time and effort is focused on attaining some level of success that is measured in stuff, money, and power. If you asked me out of college what I wanted to do, I would have told you, "I want to make as much money as possible as fast as I can." Now I consider a successful life one that is focused on doing meaningful things, living with purpose, and making a difference for others.

Don't be a victim of your suffering. All of us have experienced suffering, or will, but the good news is we have the choice and ability to overcome whatever we've experienced. Honestly, I didn't know if I would be able to survive the loss of a child. It's excruciating emotionally, mentally, and physically. There were many times when I wanted to give up.

But Jacob was one of the reasons that I decided to *not* let my pain and grief define who I am. We are made up of more than just one disappointment, bad choice, mistake, or tragedy. We all have the choice to get off the ground. We just have to choose to do it and start taking the incremental steps by putting one foot in front of the other toward hope.

You are good enough. For most of my life I've worried what other people thought about me. We all struggle with insecurities to some degree. But, it has really been an issue for me in the way I act and the way I treat people. When you boil it down, there is one question I whisper to myself that generates this fear in me: "Am I good enough?" Honestly, I still struggle with this a lot, but I'm learning that the antidote for this is *love*—love for myself and love for others (even love for people I don't like).

When I think of Jacob, I remember how much he loved people and how much they loved him. The innocence of a three-year-old has taught me a lot about how I should live as an adult. Unlike adults, toddlers aren't sizing each other up and comparing their lives to other toddlers. They aren't trying to measure up to some imaginary level they've imposed on themselves. They aren't hiding and pretending to be someone they're not in order to fit in.

The key for me is to first know that *I am enough,*

just the way I am. That's how Jacob saw me, and that's how I want to see myself—through his eyes. That allows me to love myself and accept who I am, faults and all, and it allows me to be more vulnerable and loving toward others. I would rather live a life being open and loving, risking getting hurt and disappointed, than to live a life full of fear, anger, and stress.

Even though Jacob was only three, I'm thankful for the time we did have with him. I'm thankful to be his daddy and I'm grateful for how much love he showed me.

At Jacob's life celebration, I spoke about him, about his legacy and his love. This book is another tribute to him, and I hope it honors him well. I said these words that day, and they are still true today:

Jacob Thomas Jones, you are not only my son, but my superhero.

Kelsey, Brea, Jacob, Jason, and Kendall. November 2009.

The dedication of "Jacob's House." June 2014. Murole Preparatory School. Rubanda, Uganda.

Kelsey, Jason, Brea, and Kendall. November 2014.